Toward Babel

Toward Babel

Poems and a Memoir

Ilana Shmueli

Translated by
Susan H. Gillespie

The Sheep Meadow Press
Rhinebeck, NY

All inquiries and permission requests should be addressed to:
The Sheep Meadow Press
PO Box 84
Rhinebeck, NY 12572

Designed and typeset by The Sheep Meadow Press.
Distributed by The University Press of New England.

Library of Congress Cataloging-in-Publication Data

Shmueli, Ilana.
  Toward Babel : Poems and a Memoir / Ilana Shmueli ; translated by
Susan H. Gillespie.
     pages cm
  Includes bibliographical references and index.
  ISBN 978-1-937679-02-6 (alk. paper)
  1. Shmueli, Ilana. 2. Chernivtsi (Ukraine)—Biography. I. Gillespie,
Susan H., translator. II. Title.
  PJ5054.S4598T69 2013
  892.4'17--dc23
  [B]
                                        2013020430

Contents

Child of a Good Family: Czernowitz 1924-1944

from **Leben im Entwurf**

from **Drafting a Life**

from Between Now and Now

A Toy World?
An Introduction by Gerald Stern

1.

I don't want to be carried away by either a romantic exaggeration or a mystification of the city of Czernowitz, but I can't help viewing it with a certain yearning which corresponds to the yearning—the longing—with which I view that whole Jewish world of Eastern Europe, more or less gone forever under general European onslaught, led of course by Germany, which was the head, so to speak, as Romania, Poland, Hungary, France and the others were the deadly tentacles. Romania, in particular, should be remembered, with its deep hatred of Jews, the Jews in its midst, which equaled or even surpassed the viciousness of Nazi Germany; Romania, whose first goal was, like the Germans, wholesale expulsion, whose right-wing ideologues proposed imprisoning the whole Jewish population in concentration camps and working them to death or, as one of them said, drown all of them in the Black Sea. Codreanu and his Iron Guard took over the government in 1937. This is what he said: "The Jews, the Jews, they are our curse. They poison our state, our life, our people. They demoralize our nation. They destroy our youth. They are the arch-enemies. We shall destroy the Jews before they can destroy us. . . . Every single Jew must leave this country. You ask where they should go? That is not my business."

Yet there were Jews who loved Romania, as there were those who loved Germany, Austria, Poland, Hungary and some, as we say, who were more Romanian than the Romanians, as there were those more German than the Germans, und so weiter. Czernowitz, now a Ukrainian city known as Chernivtsi, was the capital of the province of Bukovina, an important economic and intellectual center, with direct ties to the monarchy, when Romania as a whole was part of the Austro-Hungarian Empire before the breakup following World War I.

From 1870 to the Second World War Jews were the biggest population group in Czernowitz. At its peak there were 50,000 Jews, over a third. The rest was Romanian, 25%, German, about 20%, and a smaller number were Ukrainians, Ruthenians, Roma and Russians. Now the Ukranian population is 80%, the Romanian, maybe 2%, and the Jewish less than 1%. The overwhelming number were murdered, either by the Germans or the Romanians, and the rest, except for a small number, emigrated either to Israel or the United States, many, when Palestine was a British Mandate, by ship from Constanta on the Black Sea, to be interred in British camps until Israel became a state. The Jews of Czernowitz were basically German-speaking. There was an identity with the governing language of the Austro-Hungarian empire—of which Romania was a part—through a subtle identity with Austria itself, particularly Vienna, whose policies regarding citizenship, education, and the professions were, in spite of limitations and a prevailing anti-Semitic tone (sometimes more than "tone") more "liberating," especially in urban centers, than it was with the other ethnic groups in the Empire, especially in Romania itself, with its intense competing nationalisms within its constantly changing borders. It was difficult for a Jew to be an ethnic Romanian, a peasant say, even if it was—in Bucharest—somewhat easier to be a "rootless cosmopolitan" (as the Comrades termed it), speaking French and German—even when they wrote novels and poems in Romanian—and indeed were a critical part of the intellectual and political life of the country. At any rate, Romania was backward, even barbaric in its attack on the Jews, compared to the more "civilized" western countries, Germany (alas), England, France (hélas), and the United States, all of whom were critical of Romania for its Jewish policy, especially in the idyllic days leading up to the First World War and into the 1920s. These things—and more (much more)—were in the mind of Ilana Shmueli when she wrote her memoir.

2.

It is a strange memoir. For one thing it's very short, only sixty pages long, in manuscript; yet it has, in many ways, the depth, insight, and prolonged gaze of a much longer work. When you are through reading it you feel you have been involved in an elaborate detailed story and that you know that world, and its characters, as if you had spent days with them and not just the hour it took to move quickly through the narrative. It seems rough on the edges—on first reading—till you realize the language is deliberately chosen and, what is more, often acts more like the language of poetry than prose, compressed and symbolic as it is. The second chapter, titled "My Father," is really the beginning of the narrative. It is only five pages long yet it is a compendium of the entire memoir, as if everything you have to know is there. Yet, it is a series of plain—even simple (and almost simplistic)—sentences that summarize a very complex, and sometimes huge, political or family or personal situation. Just look at these sentences or short paragraphs— almost declarations:

"My father studied in Vienna. His anti-Semitic fellow students caused him to give more thought to the matter of his Jewishness. He joined the Zionist student movement Hasmonea, became a Maccabee, and fought for a new, free, and proud Judaism...As a fearsome fencer belonging to a Jewish dueling fraternity, he was infamous among the Christian students."

My parents met at the opera, fell in love, and married. My father, brought home to Czernowitz—as he told us—'the most beautiful girl in Vienna.'

My mother was never able to overcome her longing for the 'Kaiser-und Walzerreich' the empire of emperors and waltzes...But she submitted sadly and somewhat bitterly to her well-preserved life."

My beautiful mother had a profound distaste for idealism and nicotine stains.

"In the early 1930s, the actively extreme anti-Semitism of the Romanians came to our half-Jewish city. Father was physically attacked.

We were quite pretty, and yet he couldn't take proper pride in his daughters. We didn't excel at sports, were not interested in Zionism, were rather shy and awkward—and above all, we weren't boys.

He wore the yellow star on his chest with dignity."

3.

There are eighteen remaining chapters in the memoir, most of them only a few pages long. They mark the journey of a child, born in 1924 in the provincial city of Czernowitz, to her voyage to Palestine, at the age of 20, in a ship in the midst of the war, at one of the very centers of the dislocation, humiliation, torture and murder of the country's Jews. Yet it is a dream landscape because the world it describes, 65 or 70 years after the fact, has absolutely disappeared, from the landscape, from history, almost from the mind, as if if Shmueli had not painfully and painstakingly remembered it, it would never have existed.

It's as if she remembers what she chooses to remember, yet what she remembers, what she writes about, are the absolutely critical things, as if there wasn't a lot of time—and there wasn't, for Shmueli died six or so months ago, in 2011, five years after her summing up.

She remembers her "bad" grandmother from Vienna, who visited—with her husband—the spacious "villa" in Czernowitz once a year and stayed for a month, always bemoaning her beautiful youngest daughter's relocation and the Viennese life she abandoned, with its waltzes, its lofty buildings, its food, its grace—for a "hole," and she remembers grandpapa as ineffective and lazy, having affairs with the young salesgirls in his shop and smoking smelly cigars. She remembers that they were long-assimilated village Jews who paid little attention to their Jewish heritage, that her mother learned to play the piano and speak French and that her dance card was always full; long, but not too long, before Hitler, Anschluss, the war, and the yellow patches. Shmueli tells us that she day-dreamed all through school, that when she entered kindergarten she spoke German and knew only a few words of Romanian, that she met Celan at a friend's house at an early age, and that she always felt like an outsider.

The Soviets came in 1939 when she was fifteen and the Germans in 1941, when she was seventeen. Under German—and Romanian—occupation the Jews of Czernowitz were confined to a ghetto and wore the yellow star. Nonetheless, she tells us, she studied violin, learned English and even Greek, and read German authors. It was at this point that she heard Paul Celan's first poems and listened to him lecture on Villon, Baudelaire, and Rimbaud. They became close friends, though he exuded, she says, an air of ironic superiority, and she alludes to their meeting again in Paris more than 20 years later, which she tells us about in her earlier book, *The Correspondence of Paul Celan and Ilana Shmueli*, their affair, their exchange of letters and poems, her concern and care for him before his suicide.

The last four chapters are about Palestine—and Israel—her father's loneliness and sickness, her mother's dignified death, her loveless arranged marriage (through the intervention of the Ladies of Czernowitz), her own alienation—and bitterness—as an artist, a poet, a violinist, from the work ethos of early Israel. It is not an autobiography—there are a thousand unanswered questions. It's hardly a memoir. It's something else, a poem of sorts, maybe a kind of deathbed memory, free to go where the soul wants, as maybe it wants very little.

For me, Czernowitz is summoned—it is summed up—in the chapter called "Children's Birthdays." Shmueli says that her birthdays and those to which she was invited actually gave her little pleasure. But it had to do with her sensibility. She describes the food, the presents laid out on the grand piano, the artistic performances of the children, dances, theatricals, recitations. In one "celebration," the high point was the dance of the girls—four twelve-year-olds dressed identically in coy black-and-white costumes à la Folies Bergères in which they performed the little foolish dance, with the synchronized jumps and chorus girl kicks that had been drilled into them, as well as they could. "They stand before me," Shmueli says, "in order of their height, and I think of their fates, of which they could have no idea then, of ruptures, farewells, and early death." These well-bred girls from perfectly kept houses, winter gardens, and Biedermeier salons, Vienna gone mad in Czernowitz. A toy world.

from LINOLEUM

by Gerald Stern

              . . . I was
swimming south, she had castles
for thighs, there was a chain bridge
she used as a belt, she wanted
to come to America, she was a
Jew lost in Paris, she
wanted to marry me but
I was already in love with
Ilana Shmueli from Czernowitz,
a name that sounds amusing,
a city that sounds amusing
to our Anglo-Saxon ears
that hate Slavic syllables,
especially endings, she left
on the last tub from Romania—
the other two sank—and stayed
in an English concentration
camp in Palestine
and lived in Israel for sixty
more years but never learned
Hebrew properly—she studied
Greek while wearing the star
and taught herself Yiddish
since Jews from Czernowitz
mostly spoke German
as if they were in Vienna
living with lace doilies

and learned the violin
playing every day though practically
starving, she was instructed
by Paul Celan who lectured on
Villon, Baudelaire, Rimbaud,
eighteen years old already
while she was fifteen and living—
like him—in a Nazi ghetto,
and they took dangerous walks
in the public gardens
outside the ghetto;
and met him again in Paris
twenty, thirty, years later
and slept with him and listened
to his poems and tried to nurse him
and read her own to him
I spoke to by telephone
maybe a year ago
in Tel Aviv and we were
making plans for her to
come to New Jersey but then
she died and we never talked
linoleum nor double
helixes and she hated
Bibi the dangerous pedantic
fool who played football—
you won't believe it—
in high school outside
Philadelphia they called
Benny the bully, smoke that,
fact checkers for the New Republic—

I would have met her plane
and rented a Lincoln for her,
I would have given her water
then let her sleep awhile
on the way to the hotel
in Madison, New Jersey,
her first room in America.

Translator's Note

Ilana Shmueli did not start writing poetry until she was almost 50, following her late-in-life love affair with Paul Celan. They had been close as young people in Czernowitz under Russian and German occupation, and met again in Paris in 1965. The love affair took fire in October 1969 during Paul's only visit to Israel, continued in correspondence[1] and during Ilana's visits to Paris, and realistically ended with Paul's suicide in 1970. For Ilana it never ended. Certainly, Celan's ghost haunts her own poetry.

Ilana first began writing as a translator, bringing Celan's poems across into Hebrew. She listened and lived intensely with his poems, first as his lover, when he read his poems to her in Paris and sent them to her in Israel, then as his translator. Her poems return echoes of his, especially the 27 poems Celan wrote to her as part of their correspondence.

Celan inhabits her poetry: "I too have incurred your songs/ gravel under my tongue/ I stutter/ on/ toward the almond branch/ that you gave me." Almond branch, in German, is Mandelstab, which harks back to one of the first poems Paul sent her in 1969: "Almonding one, you who only half spoke." "Almond" is the lovers' code word for the shared Jewishness and common fate that for Paul lay at the core of the relationship. "Half speaking" is another code word, referring to difficulties Ilana had expressing herself in their conversations. She found her voice by reflection and refraction, speaking back to him. The cycles "My code word in you," "Leave interpretation," and "And the orphaned hands" bear the clearest evidence of this. "You come back," from the cycle "My code word in you," is a reference, almost a gloss, on several poems in the correspondence. Distressed, Ilana would travel to Jerusalem from Tel Aviv, her home at the time, to relive the brief time she and Celan spent there, including a walk around the city that Celan immortalized in poems to her.

Here is Ilana's poem:

---

1 *The Correspondence of Paul Celan & Ilana Shmueli*, 2011: Rhinebeck, NY, The Sheep Meadow Press.

You come back

try to grasp the shard
lift light from temples' depths
stride down King's roads
through bricked-over doors

And here are three of the poems Celan wrote to her, to which her
poem clearly makes reference:

THERE WILL be something, later,
it fills up with you
and lifts itself
to a mouth

from the shard-shattered
madness
I stand up
and watch, as my hand
draws the one
single
circle.
is it death, or the Promised Land?

* * *

THE SHINING, yes, that
Abu Tor
saw riding toward us, we were
orphaned in each other, with life,
not just from the hand-roots—:

A golden buoy, from
temples' depths,
measured the danger lying
silent beneath us.

* * *

THE KING'S road behind the false door,
death-surrounded
by anti-signs
the lion sign before it,

the constellations, capsized,
swamped,

you, with the eyelash
that plumbs the wound
outward.

Some of the poems in the cycle "Leave interpretation" I believe
are spoken directly to Celan. This is a remembrance that is always
questioning and seeking, never sentimental. Here, the debt to Celan is
perhaps most telling, in the attention paid to the search for meaning
through language, with its specific sensitivity to loss and mortality—
and to the ashes of the holocaust.

The place where syllables meet glows

attend to the word
its sense is not single

leave interpretation

go with the whispering under the ashes

The glow appears in the next-following poem, as well.

She does not rest
has not rested for a long time

asks, waits and listens
waits for an answer

in the darkness
behind the crack under the door
she senses a glow
does she grasp it?
Does she grasp its meaning?

The reference to a "glow" recalls the glow under the door that Celan once sensed on a visit to his aunt Bertha Antschel in London, and that came to stand, for him, for the presence of the divine, which is absent, barely perceptible in its negation whether in life or in death.

Yes, the cycle "And the orphaned hands" really does have the character of an homage, and contains several direct quotations from Celan's poems, explicitly marked as such.

Among Ilana's poems, the cycles "Never again to run against the wind" and "Let me walk across meadows" are the most autobiographical, with lyrical revelations of her childhood. The poem "Roughhousing in fresh snow" refers explicitly to the early suicide of Ilana's sister. It was particularly important to Ilana, who wanted that poem read at a Goethe Institute event in Jerusalem that she was unable to attend due to her final illness. The poem's reference to her sister's "letting go" was premonitory. Ilana died the next morning, on November 11, 2011.

In the cycles "Head full of sand" and "Cuneiform," Ilana looks at the process of growing old, with a side glance at the culture's cult of eternal youthfulness. In the first group of poems in her posthumous volume *Drafting a Life*, a cycle she titles "Homeland with no foundation," addresses the political with an equally devastating look at her two "homelands," Czernowitz and Israel.

From Czernowitz in Bukovina (now Ukraine), to Jerusalem in Israel, Ilana Shmueli experienced life as a "crossing," in German, a *Kreuzweg*, which also means via dolorosa. To translate her is to venture out along the paths she traveled, from Czernowitz to Jerusalem, where I had the opportunity to know her.

In closing, I would like to say how important it was to me to be able to review the translation of Ilana's correspondence with Paul Celan with her and Barbara Schmutzler, her invaluable friend and assistant.

The hours spent in this way provided penetrating insights into the particular diction she and Celan shared. Hannah Szpirglas, another friend in Jerusalem, Ilana's German publisher Rimbaud, and poet and translator Frank Shablewski, were important guides and interpreters.

I am grateful to the Goethe Institut in Jerusalem and its director Simone Lenz, who arranged the reading in November 2011 and supported the Lyris Circle of German Jewish emigrés reading and writing in German. (The title is short for *Lyrik aus Israel*, Poetry from Israel.) Stanley Moss is an exemplary editor of poetry, whose unerring sense of where a line goes wrong has contributed greatly to the final text of these translations. To our lasting regret, he and I were unable, in the last months of Ilana's life, to go over the translation with her.

The poems in this edition are taken from Ilana's two published volumes of poems, *Between Now and Now* (*Zwischen dem Jetzt und dem Jetzt*, 2007) and the posthumous *Drafting a Life* (*Leben im Entwurf*, 2012). They are printed in reverse chronological order, the most recent volume appearing first, following the memoir, *Child of a Good Family: Czernowitz 1924-1944* (*Ein Kind aus guter Familie. Czernowitz 1924-1944*).

—Susan H. Gillespie

Child of a Good Family

Czernowitz 1924-1944

A Memoir

Wrestling in fresh snow

blinding white as never again
and the way it melts in a child's mouth

lilacs from those days
the scent of hidden violets
fresh-mown grass
burning sunshine
dreams in the walnut tree
small green-brown fingers
on rough bark

all that – may we name it

it tugs

it tugs
at the hand of my sister
that let go so early

Czernowitz German was infamous for its "nigun[1]," its distinctive and rather unusual sentence structure—people split hairs over it, joked and teased each other, and made "Czernowitty" conversation. Even with great effort it was not possible to rid yourself of it altogether.

In the Jewish areas, Yiddish was spoken; the language was also cultivated and promoted by Bundists and Yiddishists. We had noted Yiddish poets like Itzig Manger and Elieser Steinbarg.

In our home we spoke what was—by Czernowitz standards—cultivated German.

I never learned German systematically, but always have spoken and read it.

Sometimes "back then" still echoes in my use of language. The short history of the confusing nature of my language goes like this: Romanian, French, school Latin and the Greek Alphabeth, Yiddish, also some Russian and Ukrainian, English and finally Hebrew, the language that is so important to me, the language of our country. I have never been able to master it fully, and struggle with it to this day. I stammer it, love it, but never have become as adept at it as I would like.

Frustrations, insecurities, limitations. For me, this much-lauded multi-lingualism has often meant an inability to speak. It also expresses itself as a lack of linguistic identity—a problem of identity in general.

In which language do I love, do I swear, dream, complain and pray—in what language will death come to me?

My Father

My grandfather Josef S. was a railroad administrator in a distant suburb on the border of Bukovina. He and his immediate family were the only Jews there. They had assimilated with the population of the village and completely repressed the Jewish tradition.

My grandmother Marie, rotund and beautiful, was a woman who loved life and attended all weddings and funerals with equal fervor. She owned a tavern that catered to passing travelers. My father Michael, an

---

1 *Nigun*: a wordless song. Usually performed in groups, practiced among Hassidim.

only child, was mostly left to himself. At age nine, he was sent to live with a family in Czernowitz so he could attend school there. Later, he would study in Vienna.

He never became close to the family that was assigned to take care of him. When he was sixteen, he fell in love with beautiful Wanda, the Ukrainian maid—he got close to her. One day she informed him that she was pregnant, whereupon she was let go. She moved out and supposedly had a child, although he never saw it and never wanted to see it. Nevertheless, he sent Wanda his entire allowance every month for a period of three years without complaining. Later it was somehow discovered that there was no child. Wanda claimed that it had died. My mother told me this story when I was already grown—along with other things about the family history and my father's past life. But it was at once too much and too little for me to truly get to know the human being Michael S.

I never had a chance to get to know my grandfather, who died during the First World War.

His widow Marie was amusing. We children called her the "good Czernowitz Grandmama," as opposed to the "bad Viennese Grandmama." Once a year we went with the "good Grandmama" to the grave of her "dearly departed." Prior to the ceremony, we watched her haggle with the cantor and the members of the *minyan*[2] over their fee. While the prayer was being said, she began to weep piteously, beat her breast and cry, "Josef, take me to you!" My sister and I stood there mesmerized and waited to see what would come next. All of a sudden, the weeping ceased and we saw her busily distributing cookies and schnapps to the poor, who stood around the grave. Then we went home to good Grandmama's house, where we feasted on large amounts of wondrously scented rose marmalade, sweet almonds, and ice-cold water—all before lunch! Grandmama told us old love stories and sang Romanian songs, to which she danced. She taught me to play solitaire. Everything she said and did had for us a hint of the forbidden; she seemed to have Gypsy blood!

The cemetery, at that time, was a friendly green place with tall chestnut trees. There was nothing frightening about it; after all, rather jolly things took place there! Apparently our mother, who encouraged us to go there,

---

2 *Minyan*: the quorum of Jews (usually men) over the age of thirteen who are required in order to hold a religious service.

thought it would develop our sense of family.

When I speak of "good Grandmama," I cannot help also mentioning her "gentleman friend," Mr. Wert. It was said that there was "something between them"—we children asked ourselves what that "something" might be.

Mr. Wert's appearance was well-groomed and imposing—with his white, twirled moustache, bowler, and walking stick. He liked to play cards, but he almost never let us children win. He seemed stingy—this he called "thrifty." He liked to write down moral sayings for us, in beautiful calligraphy on fine paper. Then we had to learn the sayings by heart. I still remember some of them:

> Never say I can't do that!
> When duty calls, difficult things are possible!
> Love of family makes difficult things doable!
> Practice doing difficult things!

* * *

My father studied in Vienna. His anti-Semitic fellow students caused him to give more thought to the matter of his Jewishness. He joined the Zionist student movement *Hasmonea*, became a Maccabee[3], and fought for a new, free, and proud Judaism. As a fearsome fencer belonging to a Jewish dueling fraternity, he was infamous among the Christian students. He was proud of the *Schmisse*—the dueling scars he bore above his nose and temples. We children stroked and admired them, along with the colorful medals from his student years—and the medals from the war as well! Studying was apparently a rather secondary matter, but Father did earn his doctoral degree, eventually, as a civil engineer.

In the First World War, my father became a first lieutenant. He wore his uniform with pride and dignity. Friends and good connections helped provide him with profitable lumber transactions, and he made a considerable fortune. My parents met at the opera, fell in love, and married. My father brought home to Czernowitz—as he told us—"the most beautiful girl in Vienna."

At that time many things were changing in the world politically, historically, and cartographically. My parents in Bukovina, like most Jews

---

3 Maccabee: The sports club was named for a Jewish army that rebelled against the Hellenstic tyrant Antiochus in 166 B.C.E, reconquering Jerusalem, expanding Jewish territory in Judea, and reasserting Jewish religious values.

in their circle of acquaintances, seemed to take little if any notice.

My mother was never able to overcome her longing for the "Kaiser-und Walzerreich"—the empire of emperors and waltzes. She saw herself as a victim of her love, a conviction that her own mother nourished. But she submitted sadly and somewhat bitterly to her "well-preserved life."

Meanwhile, my father fought for the realization of his dream of Jewish heroism and proud Maccabees. The battle was fought in innumerable meetings: in the Club of General Zionists, in the B'nai Brith organization, and above all in the Maccabee Athletic Club, of which, to his pride, he was elected president.

At the annual festival of sport, Father marched at the head of the Maccabees around the big stadium; he wore a white suit and the blue Star of David on his chest. He himself, however, was not a devotee of any sport. He spent a large amount of his time in smoky, depressing meeting halls and the back rooms of the cafés. At the various openings and celebrations he made long, youthful speeches.

There was never any serious talk of emigrating to Palestine, however.

We children were encouraged to take gymnastics at the Maccabees' Club and twice a week we had to learn Hebrew, but we never got beyond the first three pages of the *Ssifri hatov*.[4] During Hanukkah, I was made to declaim old Jewish epics; from time to time I presented bouquets of flowers to some Zionist personalities or others who were visiting from distant places, and said a sentence in Hebrew—that was the extent of our Jewish-Zionist education.

My father sometimes neglected his factory and his family. My mother suffered from this and the business did as well. But my father succeeded in deceiving himself and those around him, and even in convincing everyone that everything was in order. He became a chain smoker with nicotine fingers.

My beautiful mother had a profound distaste for idealism and nicotine stains; she smiled bitterly at the pointless enthusiasm and club-going, and accused my father of a "criminal waste of time," which was ruining us and also hurting our reputation.

Father's lifestyle and some of his Maccabee friends were a poor fit with Mother's exquisite, stylistically flawless Biedermeier salon. They

---

4 *Sifri hatov.* "my good book." Apparently a reference to a schoolbook teaching about the Bible.

clashed with the "lady" she wanted to present; they didn't fit in with her Vienna, which was in her blood. She felt left alone, and she usually suffered, often silently but demonstratively. Still, my parents succeeded in having a good marriage. They liked each other, called each other Putzi and Mucki. They gave big parties. Birthdays and various festivities were celebrated. My mother's delicacies were famous throughout the city.

In the early 1930s, the extreme anti-Semitism of the Romanians came to our "half-Jewish" city. Father was physically attacked.

A group of students from the Iron Guard, armed with wooden clubs, attempted to prevent my father, who had just been at the university negotiating an order for our factory, from leaving the main gate of the building. His negotiating partners wanted to let him out by the back door, but he refused. Head high, he marched through the main gate between the rows of angry students. They beat him with their sticks and hit him on the back and head; only his heavy winter coat and stiff hat prevented him from being seriously injured.

He cleaned off the blood as best he could and went home. After we had recovered from our initial alarm, mother applied an expert bandage. She was an excellent caregiver and proud of having served as a volunteer nurse in the First World War. Father was not insensitive to her fine, ironic smile, which once again called all his convictions into question: the inappropriate heroism, the involvement in the whole Maccabee business. She saw him as a man who was no longer young, who didn't want to grow up, who didn't know his limits.

They were both silent. Tongue-tied like an embarrassed schoolboy, my father stood there and wanted to explain something, then let it be. Before him also stood his two adolescent daughters, who also didn't dare to say anything. We were strangers to each other—what did we know about him, what did he know about us? The presence of the children—as so often—made him uncomfortable. Sometimes he attempted to be silly with them, to please them with little unsuitable presents, or he gave them a "thrashing," at the insistence of his wife, for some misdeed of which he knew nothing. We girls cried then, but he immediately forgot it.

There were also occasions, though, when he would invite his daughters to a forbidden treat at the fine delicatessen on the main street. This usually happened when we were walking home together. At the deli there were wonderful specialties—we enthusiastically ate our fill—before lunch! With the deli he never failed to make us girls happy.

We were quite pretty, and yet he couldn't take proper pride in his daughters. We didn't excel at sports, were not interested in Zionism, were rather shy and awkward—and above all, we weren't boys!

He saw his daughters, he saw his wife—he saw them from a great distance.

Then everything happened very quickly: his world broke apart. War, illness, Soviet occupation, German occupation. The eldest daughter, in a moment of panic, chose death. He had no idea how to grieve. At the burial ceremony he gave a confused and disturbed speech about war, politics, and the collapse of all values. He was unable to cry.

He wore the yellow star on his chest with dignity.

A chronic, humiliating illness troubled him during the last years of his life. Mother cared for him devotedly. He fought to maintain his dignity as a patient, a victim of aggression, as a Jew.

In March 1944, his strength failing, he helped a group of Jews from Czernowitz organize their flight and the difficult immigration into what was then Palestine. His efforts, on the voyage, earned him hostility rather than thanks. This, too, he bore, secure in his principles. He never complained.

When he arrived in Palestine—Zion, the promised land—he was too sick to make close ties with the country. He grew sad. It was hard for him to accept the help to which, as an old active Zionist, he was entitled. He felt superfluous, refused to accept that he had any rights, and kept his mouth shut.

Then came the time to die. At his bed sat his wife and daughter. Now he wanted to talk—to himself and to the women. He wanted to explain his life to himself. He searched for words and said that his failures were not due only to the war and persecution. He had failed to find the way. Perhaps he wanted to talk about his confusions and wanderings... to finally say that...

But immediately he was interrupted. My mother didn't want to hear anything. Her intentions were the best; she wanted to spare the last of his strength. Perhaps she also wanted to spare herself, or me, or the illusion that had once been her life.

Softly and with determination, she bade him to be silent. He kept silent; when we spoke to him again, he waved us off.

We, too, sat around his bed, silent.

And—I am still listening for the words that were unspoken.

Once a year, around the time of Passover, our grandparents from Vienna came for a visit, which lasted exactly one month.

In the big house the bulky luggage was piled in a heap. Everyone spoke loudly and tried to be glad. The grandparents seemed to feel a certain discomfort; perhaps it was the sudden transition from their modest apartment in Vienna, 2nd District, to the luxurious villa; perhaps it was the deep resentment Grandmama felt toward this provincial city, Czernowitz, on the border of Galicia, not so very long ago the easternmost outpost of the Holy Roman Empire—now part of Romania, but with its language and customs unchanged. The city of the many Jews, the *nouveaux riches*, the war profiteers—Grandmama scornfully dubbed them the "politicals," without paying any attention to the fact that my father was one of them.

She could not get over the fact that her Annerl—she usually called her Pannele, or even Panneleben, echoing a Jewish heritage she barely remembered—her Panneleben, her youngest, the latecomer in her marriage, the most beautiful girl in Vienna, who under the most difficult of circumstances had been sent to one of the most exclusive private girls' schools, now a lady of unimaginable *savoir-faire*, with her French and her piano-playing—that her child had to live in this hole. The elegant villa with its rather grand furniture and the whole panoply of ambitious features could not possibly fool Grandmama; for her, bankruptcy always lurked just around the corner.

The bad Viennese Grandmama was small and thin. She had a crumpled face that was very pale and covered with a thick layer of powder. Her thin, very white hair was so sparse that the pink scalp showed through (the only friendly spot of color in her entire appearance). Grandmama always wore black—mourning for her two eldest children: a daughter and a son who after the war had died in an epidemic of Spanish flu. (She also carried on her correspondence on black-bordered stationery.)

She had somewhat sensual but completely colorless lips that barely closed over her prominent teeth. And her black, deep-set eyes gave her a sharp, alert expression.

Everyone was standing around in the front hall, including us children, freshly scrubbed and combed, with smooth, tender faces, our holiday clothes starched and pressed. Grandmama immediately fell

11

upon us. Love-starved and unrestrained, she bedecked us with many wet sucking kisses and clasped us to her narrow, bony breast. As she did this, she kept calling out our names; she called my sister "Dolly," but for me she had embarrassingly chosen the name "Pottypie," which made being with her even more difficult for me. Finally, we fled into the next room to wipe the traces of saliva from our faces and unwrap the usually "practical," boring presents.

It was the longest, most difficult month of the year for all concerned. The "help" often felt insulted and complained, Mutti and Grandmama secretly wept, there were frequent shouting matches with no perceptible cause, and the grown-ups were nervous. Good, quiet Grandpapa was helpless to intervene. But we felt affection for him, with his full, ruddy face, the scent of the short, fat cigars more often than not in his mouth, his round potbelly, and the heavy gold chain with the watch that even played a soft melody every time the hour struck. He often went for walks with us in the Volksgarten Park, where we otherwise did not go, since we were only allowed to play in private gardens. He bought us little bottles of sweet, bubbly drinks in all possible colors, called "Kracherl," brightly colored bonbons, and little superfluous toys that immediately broke. Thus he frittered away his meager allowance. When we got home, he would have to listen to the long, fulminating moral sermons that repeatedly accused him of frivolity, of spoiling the children with "rubbish."

I don't know how, but somehow we got wind of the fact that Grandpapa, in his textile business, was "ineffective and lazy"— only thanks to the strict and clever foresight and frugality of my grandmother was the family able to lead an orderly bourgeois life and give the children an education befitting their station in life. It was also whispered that Grandpapa couldn't restrain himself from "flirting" with the young salesgirls in his shop and having "affairs" with them, but we didn't really have an idea what we were meant to think when it came to these things.

Grandmama couldn't stand the acrid smell of his cigars. She grumbled ceaselessly and exiled our poor Grandpapa—no matter what the weather—to the balcony, so he wouldn't pollute the air inside. She didn't like my father's chain-smoking either—although he only smoked long, slender cigarettes—but she controlled herself and held her tongue.

Behind the backs of the two gentlemen, she talked about "male

12

smells." Smoke, stale air in offices and coffeehouses, and the fact that men usually didn't wash themselves properly, much less take baths—she wrinkled her little nose eloquently.

My mother also inherited these sensitivities, sniffed at Papa, and wrinkled her nose. I, too, looked into this, sniffing around clothing and bed sheets, and discovered the "male smell" for myself.

Grandmama had plenty of reasons to be concerned and angry. The servants were lazy and impertinent, we children didn't respond and had no manners, my father was wasting his time with "pointless club-going" and Zionism, and my mother was too permissive with all of us. Grandmama's criticism was sharp and precise and she succeeded in convincing us all that there was something wrong with us.

We were told that Grandmama had bad nerves. At the dinner table the slightest noise would make her jump and let out a little cry, even when Mama rang for the maid. We children found it funny, but father reacted sharply and always rebuked her, telling her she could control herself if she wanted to. Grandmama was insulted. My mother darted annoyed looks at my father. Until late in the night, we could hear muffled sounds of quarreling coming from our parents' rooms.

During this time, we children always had reason to feel sorry for someone: the cook, the maid, the young lady who helped us with our homework, Grandpapa, Mutti, Papa, and sometimes our small, bad Grandmama. We were reminded to be considerate. Since Grandmama suffered from insomnia and wanted to rest during the day, we had to be quiet. For her part, she insisted that it was no use, "because I never sleep!"

But Grandmama didn't suffer only from sleeplessness. She also complained of chronic constipation, meaning that the toilets were usually occupied. In order not to make Grandmama even more nervous, we were not supposed to linger outside the door.

When the month was over, the grandparents drove off again. There was crying, and again Grandmama covered us with her vigorous, wet kisses.

For a few days my mother walked around the apartment as if in a dream, her face tear-streaked. She thought of Vienna, talked about her childhood, and spoke to us of "poor Grandmama." Once I saw her looking at an old, browned photograph; I wanted to see it too. It showed Karoline, our Grandmama. Thin as a reed, straight as a candle, she stood there, a young thing with a small, tender face, her long, thick hair gathered at the neck. She looked out seriously and questioningly, with her sensual, slightly pouting mouth and big dark eyes. She wore a dress of taffeta with a little *cul de Paris*, in the fashion of the day. One could see—she had already put some experience behind her, but almost everything lay in her future…I, too, grew sad and was on the point of crying with my mother.

* * *

Karoline was the eldest of seventeen siblings. Her parents, long-assimilated village Jews from Moravia, worked hard. They paid little attention to their Jewish heritage, only fasted on Yom Kippur and occasionally used down-to-earth Jewish expressions.

Karoline was soon called upon to help with the upbringing of her siblings and in the parental shop, the only dry goods store in town. For her, there had never been any childhood, never any youth, as she bitterly and repeatedly informed her children and grandchildren. She always had to be "strict and energetic." Soon she was married off in Vienna. The marriage was not good.

Heinrich, her husband, was easy-going; he was plump and loved the good life. He didn't talk much, but also didn't do much. He was a poor shopkeeper and took little pleasure in it. He enjoyed paying court to the shop girls, and once he was caught doing so by Karoline. From then on it was no fun for him at home. His children loved him. Naturally, he had nothing to say about their upbringing.

Karoline was compelled to keep an efficient and frugal household. The children were brought up properly, as befitted their station in life. She had a hard time with the two eldest—they were independent and rebellious, simply impossible to control. No one stood by her—she had to be very strict; it was a matter of breeding, order, and morals.

When Olga turned 18 and Oscar 17, they ran away from home. Olga became an au pair in America, and then married. Oscar went to Italy, became a journalist, and had himself baptized. Later he wrote a play that was even performed in Vienna, at the Theater in the Josefstadt. For her part, Karoline worked even harder keeping up the house. Anything made of nickel was polished daily with a special cream. She started to suffer from insomnia and chronic constipation. The First World War came, and the hunger; her two big children came back to die of the Spanish Flu. Ever since then, Karoline only wore black.

But Karoline just worked all the more intently. The floors were thoroughly waxed every day, of course. The furniture in the salon remained covered with protective doilies all year long.

As she claimed, she now stopped sleeping altogether and every evening set out four or five glasses of water and a big plate of dry biscuits, which she sipped and nibbled at during the night. She suffered from "nervous tension," started at the slightest sound, cried out and trembled for a while afterward.

Anne, or as Grandmama caller her "Panneleben," her last-born, was her consolation. Pannele was the most beautiful, the best-behaved. Only once did she give the little girl a real thrashing—when the child, during a serious fight with Heinrich, climbed onto her father's knees, caressed and kissed him. Neither of them ever forgot the incident.

Pannele received an excellent education. She learned to play the piano and speak French and was sent to the most exclusive private girls' school. She attended the great balls, and her dance card was always full. She became a proper lady. She was the only thing that remained to Grandmama; then that, too, was taken away. The dashing first lieutenant came from Bukovina—a good match, it was said—and her child moved far away, to Czernowitz. And there, too, the situation was not good.

Now Heinrich helped out around the house—went to market and did a poor job of buying groceries. There were times when Karoline, in a fit of rage, threw the purchases he brought home out the window.

Once a year, they traveled to Czernowitz, and that was no fun either.

But Karoline managed one master stroke, which people would talk about for years. In Czernowitz, "Dolly" was born, the crybaby. Grandmama was told that no one, any longer, was able to sleep through the night—despite the nurses. Then she intervened. Mother and child were ordered to come to Vienna. Already in the first night, they were separated, and Pannele was put in the farthest room. Dolly screamed for seven nights "like a stuck pig"; from time to time, Karoline looked in on her and remarked on how the baby, that clever little devil, raised her head as if to see whether someone might be coming. No one came. Pannele cried in her room, but allowed it to continue. On the eighth night, it was finally quiet. Grandmama had done it. She had vanquished the baby.

Many years followed in which nothing happened. Hitler came, then the *Anschluss*, and the war broke over them like a natural catastrophe. No more trips to Czernowitz, no visits to Vienna—there were long, hard-to-decipher letters with secret codes. The sender was now Karoline Sara... Her Judaism was finally made clear with the yellow patch and the name Sara. At Yom Kippur she fasted, as always. Heinrich fell ill and was referred to in the letters as "poor Heinrich." She cared for him faithfully. She continued to keep her household neat as a pin. Then Heinrich died.

Now she was utterly alone—the deportation order to Theresienstadt arrived. Grandmama was 86 years old and wrote in her letters that she wouldn't be "making mischief" in this world much longer.

She knew what needed to be done. She had planned and prepared everything. Sleeping pills, many sleeping pills. The apartment was in order, everything polished to a high gloss.

It was so easy—at last she would sleep—after all that...

What may she have been thinking in those hours? The little nemesis with her wasted passion, her rage at fate, her courage now to say NO and die her own death.

Kindergarten and School

Unlike the previous generation, which had still been educated in German under the Habsburg monarchy, my generation attended Romanian schools.

At five years, I was supposed to enter the Romanian kindergarten. I spoke German, with only a few words of Romanian. A few days before the first day of kindergarten, an opportunity appeared at the front door of our house. An elderly, very elegant-looking gentleman addressed me; I thought he looked "Christian." He said to me—in Romanian—"Cum te cheama. Care este tara noastra..."[5] I answered him in perfect Romanian—as it seemed to me. He stroked my hair and praised me.

Whether this event is true or I made it up, I can no longer say. My parents and the young lady who was our tutor laughed at me and claimed that everything I said was a complete lie. They simply didn't

5 What is your name? What is the name of our country?

think I was capable of it.

When I entered kindergarten, a very beautiful raven-haired Romanian woman was waiting for me. She stood in the middle of the room and asked, with a friendly smile: "Cine ma iubeste"?[6] All the children shouted: "eu, eu!"[7] They ran to her in response to the invitation. Naturally, I remained standing to one side, found it all unconvincing, and wept bitter tears of alienation. Later, when we were supposed to sing together—I can no longer remember the song—I refused to make a sound. I also never went back to kindergarten.

* * *

School had to be attended, willy-nilly. For ten long years I learned Romanian, but it always remained problematic for me. Sometimes it seems as if I have completely repressed it. I understand almost everything, but don't manage to bring forth a single word, in contrast to most of my fellow students. I remember one poem and one song. As for high school, I…slept through it.

There was a girl in my class whose last name was Maiberg. She came from a very poor family; she was ugly, poorly dressed, with oily hair, and exuded a stale, stuffy smell. But her notebooks were clean and orderly, and she knew the right answers to all the questions, was always prepared, and never daydreamed in class. From that time on, I believed that if you are poor and ugly, you have no choice but to be hardworking and orderly, and to be a good student. This would result in your having fewer problems than the "pretty, spoiled child" from a more privileged family.

It was not until my tenth year that I had my first girlfriends. Every morning I was driven to school in our small limousine (a Sandläufer), which never ceased to embarrass me. Indeed, I asked the driver to stop before we got to the school building, and got out so as not to be seen. But in the afternoon, there was the car, waiting for me in front of the school door.

So I was not accustomed to walking home with other children, strolling down the streets. I didn't dare invite one or another of the children to drive with us. I thought they looked down on me because I was so spoiled, so different. The children, for their part, found me

---

6 Who likes me?

7 I do! I do!

17

stuck-up.

School remained alien to me, and so did the children I met there. I don't remember ever playing with them in the schoolyard.

I dreamed my way through class, often laid my head on my arms and fell into a kind of half-sleep that was rich in fantasies. Whatever was being taught there did not interest me. One day the teacher had the whole class stand up softly and sing a lullaby. I noticed too late. When I wanted to stand up and sing along, he told me to stay seated and go on dreaming, for the class was singing the lullaby for me. Now I really hid my head in my arms!

Ping-pong

In the afternoon our tutor would sometimes take me to play with other children my age. These were the children of family friends. It was not always easy to keep us busy, to find games that we thought were fun.

Once I was brought to the garden of a beautiful villa. It was the home of a girl named Ruthi, who was my age, and I enjoyed going there. Ruthi received her lessons at home every day, from a teacher who came to the house; her mother was worried about "infections." Ruthi was very thin and pale, but I envied her because she didn't have to go to school. She confided to me that she thought she would have to die soon. As long as I knew her, however, she remained healthy. During the war she and her family died on the way to Palestine, in the sinking of the steamer Struma.

But on that particular afternoon, we ran around in the garden and tried to play ping-pong, not very successfully. Ruthi had a brother who was four years older, Paul; he had also invited a friend over to play, who—like him—was called Paul. Paul's guest was a strikingly handsome child, but his behavior was wild and ill-mannered, which, as Mama G. said, was no wonder, for he came from "Wassiliko Lane"— or something like that, whispered Ruthi. Paul Antschel (Paul Celan) was a model student, in contrast to Ruthi's brother, which is why he was invited.

The two Pauls were roughhousing; they made fun of us younger girls and interrupted our ping-pong. Then the boys had the idea of luring us into the cellar, where, so far as I can recall, they played forbidden games with us and did their best to scare us.

Mama G. arrived "in time," perhaps because she could no longer see us in the garden, and…"oh-my-god"—where were the little girls?… Paul, the guest, was found guilty, scolded, sent home and never invited back. He became *persona non grata*. Mrs. G. gave us a stern lecture and kept repeating how "outraged" she was.

The Children's Room

My sister was four years older, and until I was ten and she was fourteen, she and I shared a spacious, bright children's room. It had a big terrace. I can still see the delicate white-enameled furniture and the wallpaper with its repeating rose pattern, which also covered the ceiling. We were constantly told to keep everything in perfect order, not to "lounge around" on the made beds, etc. But we were not children who followed orders.

There was also a doll's room where we were supposed to play, but we were never clear about its real purpose. After we started school it was turned into a "tutors' room." Young female students from the region, who had come to Czernowitz to attend the university, came to instruct us. They were meant to help us with our homework and to keep us occupied with suitable activities in our free time. The students' circumstances were modest; they were forced to work to support their studies. Our parents' behavior toward them was "liberal" and "egalitarian."

We ate lunch together. On these occasions, fierce political discussions ensued between my father and the "young ladies." He needled them for their "leftist leanings," while they stood by their opinions—sometimes they even became fresh. The subjects were Po'alei Zion versus General Zionists[8] and socialism and capitalism. Sometimes the discussions turned into shouting matches. My mother, for whom cultivated, respectful relationships were important, became very agitated.

One especially beautiful student, whom I loved a lot, was a Communist. She told me about Communism. I listened to her with devotion and enthusiasm—eventually she was "let go." Later we had

8 *Poalai Zion*, or *Po'ale Tsiyon* (Workers of Zion), was a Marxist workers organization affiliated with the Second International, whereas the General Zionist Party was more centrist in its politics.

proper teachers who came to our house by the hour.

My sister and I, even as young children, could not accept ckass differences and developed a very strong, if not very well thought-through sense of social justice.

We felt like outsiders in the so-called upper middle class to which we belonged. The lower the social position of our servants, the more we identified with them. It did not, however, make us uncomfortable when they did things for us, for we were not obliged to do any housework. Even our homework was often done by the students, so we would finish more quickly.

In the evening, we often left the door to the children's room open so we could listen to our parents' conversations. They generally talked about their standard of living, purchases, invitations, and plans, or about the work and political activities of my father. These were topics that frequently led to serious discussions. We should learn from the example of the K. family, or the L. family, who had an overseas bank account, who traveled; the women had their clothes made by fashionable dressmakers in Vienna… We, for our part, had debts…

Occasionally, when my mother had succeeded in bringing my father to "white-hot rage" and he started to bellow, she wept loudly, gathered up her coverlet, and spent the night in the guest room.

Next day everything was fine again, just as it was meant to be. But we smiled sardonically. Once again, everything "as if"!

One night, as another fight began, my sister and I held hands tightly and simultaneously swore an oath, our voices loud and solemn: "We want to lead an entirely different life." That was as far as our imagination could take us.

An Afternoon with my Mother in the Volksgarten Park

I was five or six years old when my father's business neared bankruptcy. I didn't fully understand the word, but it was clear to me that my bad Grandmama from Vienna was right after all—we were living frivolously, far above what we could afford—was it all a house of cards?

We children kept our thoughts to ourselves.

Papa and Mutti were very worried. At that time they hardly paid any attention to us. The beautiful big villa was rented out for three years to Max, Knight of Anhauch. He was very impressive, elegant, with a monocle and a snow-white, twirled moustache—he was a converted Jew, rich and universally honored. Despite the disorder and the loss, my mother was proud that our beautiful house was rented to Max, Knight of A. This honor was her consolation. We found it all very exciting.

Before we moved into a more modest apartment, there was a transitional period and problems with the servants: Which of them was to be let go? Who should remain?

One afternoon—I didn't know why—I found myself with my mother in the Volksgarten Park. We sat on one of the benches, set around a densely planted, beautiful bed of roses. It was the first time I had visited the park with my mother. I was familiar with it because occasionally one of the maids would take me to the Sunday morning "promenade."

It was also the first time that I had spent an afternoon with my mother alone and not at home—and that in the Volksgarten Park! I was anxious, didn't know how I was expected to behave...The feeling of down-heartedness was familiar to me and made me afraid. At home I made light of it by running circles in the big dining room and singing to myself: "I am soooo booored—sooo boored!" Here in the out of doors, alone, I simply stood around and didn't know what to do next.

My mother sat on the bench, sad and alone. I felt sympathy for her, but didn't know what to say and remained silent, which was also unusual. Finally I went to her, to ask her what I should do. She told me I should play with the children, who were enjoying themselves with hoops and badminton, hopscotch and cookies. Unknown children, games that I knew, to be sure, but didn't enjoy. My mother suggested that I pick out a girl, tell her my name, and ask: "Girl, what's your name? Would you like to play with me?"

But I felt shy about pronouncing my name; my nickname was "Schnipsi," or "Schnipserl," which never failed to embarrass me. (It insults me even today to be called that. I finally got rid of the name in Palestine.)

The whole plan took a catastrophic turn. I did everything my mother had suggested—but I decided to call myself Erica. For me, Erica was a proper, normal name—the kind of name girls should be called.

The girl said: "I don't know you; I don't want to play with you."

When my mother saw me withdrawing, insulted and alone, she called: "Schnipserl, come to me!"

The children broke into laughter and made fun of me: "Schnipserl! Schnipserl!"

Mortified, we left the park.

The ladylike, almost regal superiority of my mother, which at the time I admired a lot, was shattered for me.

Conversations with Myself

Until I entered the Gymnasium in seventh grade, I never had any girlfriends. I played by myself, spent a lot of time sitting in the kitchen, listening attentively to the endless conversations of the "help," interrupted my sister and her friends in their secretive doings, and found no place and nothing to do for myself. Sometimes I danced around in my room and sang rhymes to myself, or carried on private conversations that I for the most part found amusing. There were euphoric moments as well. Then I ran around in circles and sang, "I love Mutti. I love Papa. I love Dolly. I love the whole world so much—aaand—the whole world loves me." I dreamed I was a queen in disguise, dreamed of great grown-up parties with innumerable extraordinary guests who never bored me and whom I invited to stay with me forever... After the real guests had gone home I also loved to empty the remains of the sweet liqueurs from their little crystal goblets. Then, lost in a dream, I told myself stories.

We were now living in a temporary apartment; my room was next to that of my parents. One afternoon—my father was no longer going to the office—I was once again deep in conversation with myself, when suddenly my father opened the door and stood before me, pale and staring at me with a horrified expression.

"You are alone? You are talking to yourself? For God's sake, child, are you mad?" he asked.

What is mad, I asked myself; I had only a vague idea. Mad was the meschugge red-haired Hoita-Poita, whom we always ran from as he careened through the streets crying "Hoita-poita." We laughed, but were very afraid of him.

Was that mad? So I am...mad?

My father continued: "Only people who are mad talk to themselves! You must promise me, on your holy word, that you will never talk to yourself again!" He patted my hair, walked out of the room and left me alone. I cried quietly to myself for a long time and asked myself: What is mad?

The Marriage Beds

My parents' marriage beds were carved from light-stained walnut and artfully decorated with gold-colored metal; they filled most of the room. The cushions and bed curtains were of a pale violet color, as were the silky, feather-light down quilts. My mother's bed had a barely perceptible scent of perfume: "Crèpe de Chine." It came in an elegant little bottle in a grey velvet mesh. This little bottle made me think of a charmed, fairy-tale image of Paris.

I quickly learned to lie my way into my mother's bed using made-up illnesses. I know that my mother liked to sit by sickbeds and was a dedicated nurse. So I cleverly simulated all kinds of infirmities: flu, stomachache, indefinable temperatures and headaches. On such days my mother, who was generally very strict with me, let me lie in her great soft bed, and turned down all social obligations in order to sit by me and spoil me.

Thus I managed to dream away the greater part of my school years. The great bed saved me from long hours in the bare, chilly schoolrooms with the teachers I didn't like and the Romanian language I never became intimate with; from the shame of being caught not knowing the multiplication table, or moving my lips soundlessly during choral singing—although my hearing was good, I sang hopelessly off key. My mother's marriage bed saved me from boring piano lessons and private French lessons, from the difficult gymnastic practice at the horse and parallel bars in the Maccabees' Club, where we ran around in circles and marched (I always got off on the wrong foot!). It saved me from the grotesque dancing school, that—in my eyes—ridiculous swooping around and graceful fluttering of hands…and it also saved me from ice-skating.

I lay in the magic bed and created my Nirvana. At age six, I announced to everyone who would listen that I was going to study "genius." (The word "genius" was much in vogue in Czernowitz at that time.) I saw myself as a tightrope-walker, bareback-rider, storyteller; as good and bad fairy and as a great healer who helps all children, understands their pranks, and safeguards their secrets. Lying in this bed meant security for me. I called it "horizontaling." I "horizontaled" in order not to have to be upright, to stand up in front of others in an alien world that didn't suit me in the least.

The Bookcase

I remember a beautiful, black, carved bookcase—was it ebony? Tall and broad, it stood in the Gentlemen's Room and was usually kept locked. There stood the gold-lettered volumes of the classics—new, pristine, untouched. There was a section with Judaica: Graetz's *History of the Jews*; Herzl's *Alt Neu-Land*, etc. We had no Bible in the house.

I also remember three or four books—my mother's favorites. There were *Marie Antoinette* by Stefan Zweig and Tolstoy's *Anna Karenina*, with which she identified for reasons that remained vague to me. And there was a book with clear, "enlightening" explanations: *The Perfect Marriage* by Van der Velde. We children got a copy of the key and read it secretly. And there was another book that I loved, *The Little Barefoot Girl* by Auerbach. The poverty and simplicity of village life were very appealing to me, and I wanted to live like the little barefoot girl. Auerbach, who was unusual among Jewish writers in that he wrote novels about village life, was popular at the time. Other than that, I was regularly given the *Garden Bower* (*Gartenlaube*) monthly to read. My mother read popular novels from the lending library, my sister read hardly anything at all, and my father read all the newspapers.

But there was also a torture that involved reading: *Les Malheurs de Sophie* by Mme de Ségur, the little red volumes with which my old Madame Deschamps bored me. She had been my French teacher since the time I was five, with a white moustache that I stared at the whole time and that rendered me quite unable to concentrate.

But how should I summarize the education and culture of our little world, or make judgments about it? Certainly, I am a little bit unjust, but not too terribly. Until I was 16, I dreamed, made fun of school, of the Maccabees, of my sister's crushes and her silly friends. I found my teachers ridiculous. And other than in the kitchen and in my mother's bed with my simulated illnesses, life seemed to me extremely unenjoyable and uninteresting.

The elaborate birthdays, to which I looked forward again and again with exaggerated hopes, were always a disappointment.

My birthdays and those to which I was invited actually gave me little pleasure.

There were elaborate preparations and much effort went into drawing up the invitation list, so that no one who deserved an invitation would be left out.

Then came the question of what the children would be served. It became an actual competition among the mothers—which one would have the most beautiful, most delicious and artfully prepared tasty little aspic preparations, the fanciest *petits fours* and big, festive birthday cake with candles?

The presents were always the same, always the same games, like Parchesi, card games with educational content, and books that I didn't really want to read at all, or practical gifts from the "aunties." Everything was laid out in a display on the grand piano.

The main thing was to think of special and impressive programs for the children—to imagine performances and realize them successfully. It should be an "artistic" program in which the children themselves presented something: dances, theatricals, recitations. The choice of program reflected the taste and wishes of the mothers, who usually acted as the directors. The children were supposed to perform nicely, smile sweetly, and not forget their lines. I cannot remember having much fun doing it.

The mothers were generally nervous and tense, and I often thought, cynically, that it was more about the mothers than the children.

I remember one birthday in particular at Aunt Flora's (we usually called our friends' mothers "aunt"). Aunt Flora was especially particular about everything. It was supposed to be a fairytale, in which I played the part of a queen, but my entire role consisted of three words: "Let it be!" I was meant to speak them clearly and forcefully following a long monolog by the king. I was the youngest, it is true, but I was insulted by the small part, since I knew all the parts by heart and could declaim them faultlessly.

But the high point of this celebration was the dance of the "girls"—four twelve-year-old "sweethearts," all dressed identically in

25

coy black-and-white costumes à la Folies Bergères—still visible today in the old photograph. They performed the little, foolish dance, with the synchronized jumps and chorus-girl kicks that had been drilled into them, as well as they could. The four girls made great efforts, tried to be graceful. Their forced, well-bred smiles are visible in the old black-and-white photo. They stand before me in order of their height and I think of their fates, of which they could have no idea then, of ruptures, farewells, and early death.

The first from the right: Alice, the birthday girl. A pretty, blond, blue-eyed girl, tall and slender, she was supposed to become something special, as her strict mother had decided. The latter was a beautiful, tall, buxom woman with porcelain-blue eyes and clear skin. Always a bit frustrated, she had great ambitions for herself and her small family. (It was rumored that she demanded of her husband that he should be freshly shaved, when he…)

Alice was the only daughter.

She was not sent to school, but had a private teacher and took tests every year in Vienna. Her mother considered her to be very musical. Every morning she had to practice piano for three hours.

In the winter she was made to skate in circles for hours in her short, red skating costume sprinkled with white pearls, in the area of the skating rink reserved for figure skaters.

Alice felt the cold. She froze at the piano, and she froze at the skating rink. She often complained of frostbite. It was said that her efforts were average, something Aunt Flora, for her part, did not accept. The ambitions for her daughter knew no bounds.

The late 1930s. Hitler. The threat of war. But Alice had to stick to her training program. She remained well-bred and docile.

She married at 18. It was a marriage of convenience. During the year of the Soviet occupation she was deported to Siberia with her husband and parents.

There she died, at age 18, of breast cancer.

It is difficult for me to go on writing about the fates of the other girls.

Yiddish School—Soviet Occupation

When the Soviets occupied Czernowitz in 1939, the bourgeois world broke apart for my parents. My father was spied on and persecuted as a Zionist and a capitalist; his shop and work were expropriated. He became unemployed. We lived in two small rooms, which we subleased. But the Soviet occupation also freed us young people from the "bourgeois, petit-bourgeois oppression" that had hemmed us in.

Since the Soviets supported the idea of cultural autonomy, under their occupation there were three schools, i.e., three linguistic possibilities to continue studying: Moldavian (Romanian), Ukrainian, and Yiddish. I chose Yiddish, partly out of protest against my parents, but also because I had the completely false notion that it would be easier for me than the other languages. I thought it would suffice if I just twisted the words and spoke them with a Jewish accent—what we called "mauscheln"—as we sometimes did just for fun. I barely remembered the Hebrew alphabet, which is also used in Yiddish, since I had run away from compulsory Hebrew classes, feigned sickness or not paid attention. Most of the other students came from circles connected with the "Bund"[9] and already knew Yiddish.

At the Yiddish school, we had wonderful teachers. Our Yiddish teacher was an excellent, enthusiastic philologist who had attended the Yiddish Academic Institute in Vilnius and studied German in Berlin. Soon after I enrolled in the school, when I mangled a word in response to a question, he thought I was being fresh and making fun of the Yiddish language. With great feeling, he spoke of the beauty, richness, and magic of the Yiddish language, and how people like me drag it through the mud and disfigure it. I felt confused and hurt, but at the same time I was deeply moved by his words. I wept bitterly, and he realized his error. During recess, he called me in for a conversation. I told him where I came from, and he understood my complete ignorance...

It was the beginning of a deep, unusually rewarding friendship. Chaim Ginninger not only had knowledge, depth, and a love of language, but he was also a teacher through and through. He gave me a little book of short stories by Isaa L. Perez, with the assignment to learn to read the first story fluently by the end of the week. I was to feel every word and repeat every sentence until I could read and understand it without difficulty; during the week I was not to work on

---

9 The Bund was a Jewish workers organization founded in Vilnius 1897. It was active throughout the following decades in Lithuania, Poland, and Russia. The Bund was actively socialist and anti-Zionist in its politics; it supported Yiddish and culture and arts and was opposed to the revival of the Hebrew language.

anything else. It was the story "Dos Fuss-Schemele." A simple, pious woman is given a wish and asks God to make her the footstool of her deceased husband—in heaven. The style of the story was naïve and touching, although there was certainly more to it that I can recall today. A week later, I read the story aloud to my teacher, fluently and joyfully.

It was like an awakening. I began to look and see; poetry, music, and nature came alive for me.

The stories by Perez and the fables and parables of Elieser Steinbarg appealed to me. The first Yiddish poem I read was "Der Roich und die Chmare." I understood it, and it spoke to me from the heart. I was amazed, moved, and never forgot it. The smoke, which was once a shade-giving tree that was turned into firewood, rises to heaven and meets a cloud. It warns the cloud about the earth, tells her what awaits her there. But the cloud refuses to rise up to heaven with the smoke. The smoke pleads with the cloud:

> Kum mit mir ahin, ahinzu zu die stern
> reine finkelech, neschumelech un gufn!
> sei nor wi sei winken, wi sei rufn!
> nein! Ich ken nit! Ich arop, arop ich mis mich kern.
> Kind farwos? –ich hob a harz mit bliz, mit diner, un mit trern!

> Come up with me, up to the stars—
> pure sparks, little souls without bodies!
> Just look how they wave, how they call out!
> No, I cannot go! My path goes down, down.
> Child, why?—I have a heart full of lightening, thunder, and tears.

Thus I discovered how it is possible to "say"—to make poetry. The verses that spoke to me I have never forgotten. Many fables and parables followed, perhaps even better ones, with a lot of wit, depth, and poetry. I read the ballads of Itzak Manger about Baal-Schem Tov, along with works by Leiwick Halpern, A. Lutzki, and other Yiddish poets. I learned Yiddish songs, and wanted to accompany the melodies on the violin. Thus, I began to learn to play the violin.

Unfortunately, I did not continue with Yiddish and therefore forgot some of it. But the turning point remained and gave me, above all, love and respect for language and the word.

* * *

On the night of June 12, 1940, the Soviets carried out a large-scale deportation to Siberia, which the officials termed a "resettlement." Our family was also on the list of those to be deported. Aware of the danger, we hid. My father and my sister were concealed at a hospital by doctor friends. My mother and I found shelter with friends we thought would not be in danger. But they were picked up, unexpectedly, and we were sent away. Because we had no place else to go for shelter, we went home, where the militia was already waiting for us. We were taken to the freight yard, where the deportees were being herded into cattle cars.

For three whole days, the freight cars stood in the railroad yard. It was a terribly hot June—more than forty young and old people, thirsty babies and sick people together in the car. There was a hole in the middle of the floor with a funnel, where we were supposed to relieve ourselves. Twice the soldiers allowed me to go with a thirteen-year-old boy to fetch water for the people in the freight car. We were so happy at the fifteen minutes of freedom we were given, at the light and the air, that we laughed and sprinkled water on each other in high spirits.

On the third night, shortly before the train departed, my mother and I were let go, thanks to a surprise intervention. I left the car with a heavy heart. I experienced this "barely escaping" as a betrayal of those who were forced to leave, among them the happy thirteen-year-old.

Two thousand eight hundred people were deported from Buko-vina at that time. Many of them died in Siberia of cold and hunger, or were decimated by the hard labor.

Under German-Romanian Occupation

Summer 1941: the German-Romanian occupation. Executions, the yellow star, ghetto, mass deportations to Transnistria. The dark, wide line of people all crowded together, each with his bundle, being driven through the streets. Again, the piercing feeling of guilt for those favored ones who were able to save themselves with papers procured with the help of money, protection, or luck.

After the big deportation, the Jews lived in a closed-off part of the city; they had to wear the yellow star and were under curfew except for two hours a day. Later, the measures were made even stricter, and there were new deportations.

But in these very years, at the edge of the great destruction, we—a little group of friends—succeeded in creating a magical anti-world. There were clandestine meetings, stolen hours; we read Spinoza, Nietzsche, Rilke, Trakl, Stefan George, Karl Kraus and on an old gramophone we listened to Beethoven symphonies. With us were Chaim Ginninger and Hersch Segal, the teachers I knew from the Yiddish school. They were teachers with great knowledge, who continued to introduce us to the Yiddish language, literature, and poetry. Others joined them and through them I learned how to learn. It was absurd in that hellish time. Paradoxically, it was precisely at that time that I learned to know and love German poetry and literature.

Paul Antschel's (Paul Celan's) girlfriend at the time, Ruth Kraft, was a member of our circle. Later, she would help publish his first poems, written in Czernowitz. There was also Edith Horowitz, later Silbermann, a translator and scholar of German literature, who also published memories of Celan. Paul was often with us and read his poems to us. We spoke and read mainly German and didn't think about the fact that it was the language of the people who were annihilating us. During this time I was greatly encouraged by my teachers—these were the apprenticeship years of my life.

Rose Ausländer, who had spent a few years in America, taught me English. She had a serious, expressive face and very large, black, sad eyes. Rose Ausländer's manner was enthusiastic, exalted; at other moments she would exude solemnity and tragedy. I cannot remember any laughter, and I often found our encounters burdensome. We read poems, among others, by Keats, Shelley, and Wordsworth, which I learned by heart and for which I made up melodies.

Paul Antschel, who had an excellent command of French, read me Villon, Baudelaire, and Rimbaud. On our forbidden walks together he taught me a lot about flowers and stones.

There was also a famously strict Latin teacher from the former Gymnasium, with whom I translated Latin and Greek texts. But above all, I loved the violin.

It was in these very inhumane years that I discovered new aspects of Czernowitz—values and subjects of which I had suspected nothing during my well-protected childhood.

The Violin Teacher

Winter 1943. We are shut out—with the yellow star. It was in that situation that I discovered and "invented" music for myself—music, with which I played myself past the boundaries. I learned to play the violin.

The elderly Romanian teacher seemed like a miracle—from another world, without the Jewish Star. I never found out how or for what reason he turned up in Czernowitz.

It was freezing, the snow piled high; the elderly teacher wore a long bearskin coat, which had been given to him, many years before, by Queen Maria—this was what he said. He had a lot to say, a lot of stories, and brought with him big photo albums containing numerous pictures of him with the composer Enescu and other famous artists. Enescu was his teacher, and it was said that he had performed with him.

Florescu, my teacher, had once been very handsome and famous. Even now, he was still impressive, but he neglected his appearance; his unkempt white hair hung down to his shoulders.

In me he saw a future artist, and he sometimes succeeded in getting pure notes to emerge from my untrained fingers. During our lessons, the world did not matter to us. No dangers, no misery, no fear. He saw the enthusiastic, expectant, and eager girl before him; I saw the elderly artist, who brought music and something of the great world of the past into my room.

We played duets…He called me "Saint Cecilia" and had several photographs taken of me…He wrote me a weighty "apprenticeship letter," in calligraphy, in which he revealed artistic secrets. He drew up special exercises and transposed pieces that I especially loved into easy versions for the violin. For example, Schumann's *Träumerei*, which was new to me at the time and which I found especially moving and absolutely wanted to play. Tirelessly, we worked on it. Old Mr. Florescu managed to get me to perform it without any mistakes and with the most beautiful sound of which I was capable.

The concert took place in the morning, in the hours during which there was no curfew. I invited my friends and teachers, to whom I owed this so special violin teacher, to our house. My mother prepared a tray with little rolls—this was quite unusual for that time. She smiled at us a little, for she found the entire performance comical and inappropriate:

"You don't have anything else to worry about?" But she made us feel at home and comfortable, as best she could.

But I forgot all inhibitions, my stage fright and my mother's irony. I had been seriously studying the violin for barely two years; my sound was still unsure. But I absolutely had to perform!

For me, the *Träumerei* was my own creative idea. I wanted, I had to share it with the people who were close to me, to communicate it to them. I wasn't interested in whether they really wanted to hear it. Everyone was there, naturally my teacher among them!

In a corner stood Paul Antschel—as so often, he exuded an air of distance and ironic superiority. I took no notice of this, although I cared a lot about his listening. I played; I didn't care whether I played badly or well. I forgot everything around me, followed every note. Nothing else mattered, and it succeeded. The impossible succeeded—against all rational sense, in the winter of 1943—in a room—in the Jewish quarter—in Czernowitz.

Ginninger and Segal, who guided and accompanied me at the time, had tears in their eyes that they didn't even attempt to conceal. Florescu wept.

Never again have I experienced such profound self-forgetfulness.

Twenty-one years later, when I met Paul again in Paris, he said, interrupting our recollections—we were deep in thought, "You know, I immediately tore up that beautiful photo of you with the violin. It really went too far at the time. I could not bear the pointlessness of it."

The Forbidden Walk

A surprisingly brilliant spring day in late November 1942.

Despite the prohibitions and dangers that hung over us, Paul and I decided to brave the Volksgarten. Impelled by high spirits, we buried our yellow stars deep in our coat pockets and felt free.

We wanted to see the park's majestic, broad allee of chestnut trees again.

We strode through the thick, fragrant fall leaves and, to our surprise, we found little spring flowers sprouting: violets, forget-me-nots, primroses, and clover—we bound them into a little bouquet, put

32

them in Paul's blue peaked cap, and placed them under the old willow by the pond. It seemed to us to be the proper burial place for the spring flowers that had lost their way—for the gift of the spring day—in this autumn, these horrific days.

We recited poems into the utter stillness—our voices were too loud—.

They were lines from Shakespeare's sonnets, which Paul was already translating at the time and knew by heart: "How heavy do I journey on the way" and "Like as the waves," and, and...

What did these first translations sound like?

We also saw a tiny blooming rose on a dry stem; spontaneously we both started to sing, "'Tis the last rose of summer." But that was too silly even for us, and we laughed. Our unrestrained laughter made us feel shy—.

Then we strode solemnly down the chestnut allee—and the chestnuts bloomed a second time—white candles against the improbably profound blue of the sky.

Beautiful!

> *Whoever with his eyes has gazed on beauty,*
> *as of that moment is consigned to death.*
> *He will no more be fit for earthly duty,*
> *and yet will tremble at the thought of dying.*[10]

Which of us spoke those words back then? I have forgotten. But the verses were spoken...

Then we fell silent.

Later Paul said to me: "Chestnuts blooming again in the fall—it is a mortal illness"...

The Request

At seventeen, sixteen, I already had experienced a lot of farewells and death: my sister and my girlfriend, two people who were very close to me, had taken their lives. I understood, I didn't understand—I asked and didn't ask why it had to be that way...

---

10 The verses are from a poem by August von Platen. In German: *Wer die Schönheit angeschaut mit Augen/ ist dem Tode schon anheimgegeben.* The translation here is by Herman Salinger.

33

In the midst of it all, I nevertheless felt the expectations and longings of a seventeen-year-old girl. Their recklessness scared me, and I found them sinful at such a time. Then I came across a little anthology by Jean Paul: *The Everlasting Spring*.[11] I read and found the text "New Year's Wish for Myself," from the novel *Siebenkäs*. In it, I found an answer to my impermissible dreams, which I actually didn't want, with the result that I believed I had to free myself of them. What I read showed me a way—something like a consolation:

"—The year which has fallen to dust deals out the days according to their lot. What dost thou pray for, Nathalie?

"—Not for joy… what shines upon us is the ray reflected from the sword which the coming day will hold to our happy hearts. No, no; I pray not for joys; they make the thirsting heart so void. It is but sorrow that can fill it full.

"—Fate deals the days according to their lot. What dost thou long for, Nathalie?

"—Not love. … Ah! do not enter that bright glittering cloud—it is but mist and tears. No, no, … sink into the chill of death under a nobler poison-tree than is the lovely myrtle.

"—Thou art kneeling at the feet of Destiny, Nathalie; tell him thy desire!

"—Neither do I desire more friends. No; we stand all, side by side, on undermined graves—and when we have long held each other so fondly by the hand, and so long suffered together, our friend's empty mound caves in, and he turns pale, and sinks—and I am left alone, my life all frozen, beside the filled-up grave.

"—Oh! thou bereaved and widowed Nathalie! what would'st thou have on earth?

"—A grave, and patience; nothing else beside. But these deny me not, thou silence-keeping Fate! Dry thou mine eyes, then close them! Still my heart, then break it!"

When we fled, I left the little book behind with many others. I often thought of these lines. Later, I found an identical volume in a German used bookstore in Tel Aviv. Then it too disappeared. I looked

---

11 Jean Paul: *Flower, Fruit and Thorn Pieces: or the Married Life, Death, and Wedding of the Advocate of the Poor, Firmian Stanislaus Siebenkäs* (2 volumes; Leipzig: B. Tauchnitz, 1871), trans. by Edward Henry Noel.

34

for it for a long time, then gave up, but did not forget it.

Recently, when I was clearing out old books to give away, I found the little book again, bound in bright blue cloth, with old Gothic type, illustrated with tender ink drawings…touching, all-too touching…And yet: there was the profound, shattering knowledge of renunciation—and—the great question asked of fate. The seventeen-year-old had understood.

In Palestine

March 1944.

We have managed to run away from the persecutions, the dangers of war and occupations. We have survived the risky, mortal dangers of the boat trip from Constanta to Istanbul, the transfer to Palestine, the quarantine in the English military camp…

We have arrived!

My father sick and helpless, my mother confused and helpless, and me with my twenty years—clueless, dependent, removed from reality, and helpless…

And yet despite all that—nevertheless—the unrealizable expectations addressed to the place that would now become my homeland.

A rich uncle from Egypt—my father's cousin—had a weekend house in an orange grove. He gave us shelter there and financial support. It was a magnificent spring—the bursting, intoxicating scent of orange blossoms—well-cared for lawn and brightly colored flowerbeds in front of the small, elegant villa. However, this assistance, basically, stood in the way of a realistic adjustment that would have helped us to adapt. The true problem remained unclear; necessary solutions were put off and finally rendered impossible.

My father's Czernowitz friends and fellow party members, Zionists and Maccabees, who had come to Palestine early on, were concerned about us, but we relied on the rich uncle. They were impressed by the lovely weekend house in the orange grove—where my parents, left alone despite the material assistance, were not up to the daily difficulties.

The small town in which we lived had been founded by hardworking recent German immigrants who raised chickens. Disciplined and sober-minded, they had little sense for the luxurious properties of my Egyptian uncle and his recently-immigrated relatives from Bukovina, even though we also spoke German.

And I—I wanted to get away, to the city; I wanted to play the violin, to study music, to go to concerts, learn, learn, and..."live my life." The responsible authorities made it clear to me, with no ifs and buts, that Jews in Palestine had to work hard—everything else was a luxury. I was supposed to go to a Kibbutz...

But I wanted to play the violin, wanted music...

In the end, they found a place for me to live in Tel Aviv, in a home for young single women (*Beth Hachaluzot*). The condition was that I take a course in caring for babies. The course was supposed to last a year. At the time it seemed to me like an eternity—I did it reluctantly. But I was allowed to continue to play the violin.

My surroundings, the tone and mentality of the people I met, the home and the course, often led me to become bitter and unjust.

In the evenings, I practiced the violin in a little laundry room on the rooftop. It was humid and hot; in the sticky warmth my playing often sounded pathetic to me. But I also had moments of deep thought and new experiences.

I had no desire to work or learn what the course offered. I did poorly and was sent away with a friendly nod. The same thing occurred at other workplaces. Work didn't seem to want to succeed, for me, and I whiled away the time, incompetent and inattentive. I was useless when it came to practical work—without discipline, spoiled, soft, dreamy and full of fantasies. I waited for a miracle.

My parents and their friends from Czernowitz began to be concerned about my future.

In fall 1945, my seriously ill father died his death.

The Czernowitz Community Arranges a Marriage

My mother, who no longer could or wanted to live by herself in the distant town, came to Tel Aviv; there she had to care for an elderly, ill woman, with whom she was allowed to live. She felt ashamed; for her the experience of having to work for someone was demeaning.

Her woman friends from Czernowitz, who led orderly lives, also viewed her situation as inappropriate and felt pressured. Concerned about their own peace of mind, they wanted to know that we were well taken care of. Thus, they decided to find a good, socially appropriate "match" for me. This was the only answer for two penniless women. So…I should get married.

And I? I wanted to play the violin, study music, and go to concerts—and sometimes I also had an irrepressible desire for a particularly delicious meal, for fine dishes in an elegant restaurant. (It was the time of ration cards, of very strict rationing; the meals at the home were tasteless.)

At some point I met the man. He was more than ten years older than I and already considered a "confirmed bachelor." The Czernowitz ladies had done their research on him and were highly satisfied with the results.

He was wealthy, from a good family. He owned an elegant shop— by the standards of the time—for men's hats, imported Borsalinos, which—for reasons that were inexplicable to me—impressed the Czernowitz group. I was interested neither in the Borsalino hats nor in the business. The shop's interior had been decorated by an architect; I scarcely took any notice of the very polite and friendly man.

On the other hand, I was very happy with his generous invitations to fine, expensive restaurants, where I fell upon the delicious dishes, of which I had long been dreaming, with the enthusiasm of a starving person. Then we went to the movies. I returned to the home tired and full.

At the time, a seminar for aspiring music teachers had been funded. It was suggested that I should study there. The idea pleased me a lot.

Mr. R., who by then had fallen deeply in love, and who enjoyed giving gifts, wanted to marry me. He promised to take care of the education I so deeply desired and to provide more music lessons. In addition, he would buy a piano. He also loved music; as a child he had wanted to be a violinist, but he was not allowed to play. He promised me and my mother a "safe" home. When I told him that my feelings for him had nothing to do with love, he comforted me by saying that that would take care of itself.

The Czernowitz community was happy to see me married off and my mother taken care of, and took pride in preparing the marriage for us. They did it tastefully and also arranged for entertainment; there were witty sketches. In addition, some talented immigrants were invited to provide cultivated music-making. It was a pretty little wedding; everyone was in a good mood and satisfied.

I was apathetic, smiled a forced smile, and saw everything around me as if through a telescope, the wrong way around. Everything was small and far away. That wasn't me under the chuppah—it was a completely different young woman.

The man, sensitive and reserved, was and remained a stranger to me, unreal.

In the spacious new apartment, furnished by the architect, my mother ran the household. In the neighborhood she was known as "Mrs. R."

I studied, practiced piano and violin, attended the seminar and led my own life. At home, my mother and I divided up the roles in the marriage. My mother was happy.

The Czernowitz ladies came to the usual snacks, the Rummy and Bridge games; a good time was had by all. From time to time, there were little receptions, and often our guests forgot how far away they were from Czernowitz.

Everyone supposed that I was satisfied. And why not? After all, I had what I desired. Two years later, when I told the "good" man that I had to leave him after all, he said, with feeling: "And do you know what you are doing to your mother?"

Deep in my unconscious, I felt how profoundly I had hurt this man. But I didn't let it surface. Who was responsible, I asked myself? All that couldn't really be "me." Was it Czernowitz? Was it my mother? Was it fate?

And the ladies?

"Ach, shame—the poor mother—the poor, stupid child—they were so well taken care of!"

The Last Voyage

The young, strong male nurse arrived. He looked down at the woman's small, shrunken form, and did without the stretcher he had brought with him. He lifted her without difficulty and carried her in his arms down the four stories to the ambulance that was waiting below.

My mother was wearing a new, blue-and-white-flowered dressing gown, which she had coveted. It was warmly padded and quilted. She was very proud of it. She had also asked me to wash her thoroughly, comb her with care, and put on new underwear. Finally, she felt ready for the trip. She was satisfied.

It had been more than three months, during which she had refused to take any nourishment. Since then, she had scarcely left her bed. She dragged herself to the bathroom with difficulty, but refused all assistance.

Most of the time she was disturbed and confused, mixed things up, barely knew who she was, and only rarely recognized us. But there were occasions when she suddenly—with a sly laugh—took part in a conversation and acted as if she knew about everything. It was clear to her and us that it was a game.

Now she may not have known where she was going—but she seemed to believe that it was a great, important voyage, and she looked forward to it. She pressed herself against the friendly young man, felt a little bit ashamed, and laughed. One could see that she felt protected and secure. She said: "Look how light I am. He carries me like a child!" Her voice sounded happy, as if she were relieved that she was finally rid of the extra pounds that had weighed her down for so many years, that she could finally be the tender child, in need of protection, who was hidden inside her heavy body.

The bed in the hospital was by a window. Again, she was happy. She, the person who was perennially disappointed, who always felt at a disadvantage, now had a good bed and was thankful. She said: "Look, I have a place by the window. When I go, I will see the landscape."

Before she took her final leave from everything around her and turned away, she hugged me and said, "You unknown nurse, you were so good to me."

In this moment of her confusion—or was it illumination?—she took the oppressive burden of guilt from me; she gave me the space. I was free and close to her as never before.

There lay the starved, eighty-six-year-old little body. I saw the beautiful, blonde, well-behaved child of her mother, which she remained all her life. A child that was waiting for the big reward—and the reward never came.

Now death came, and he was generous. It was a gentle, considerate departure. Her hand stroked mine very lightly, as if by accident.

I saw her life: denial, suffering, tragedy.

Czernowitz—the farewell from the parents and from Vienna; the role of the model lady, the elegant villa with the Biedermeier salon, with its dormer windows and winter garden, the perfectly kept house.

War, Soviet and German occupation, the collapse of her accustomed life—unimaginable. During this time, she lost her eldest daughter.

But in the most difficult situations my mother showed astonishing courage, imagination, and vital strength. In the train car to Siberia, in the ghetto, where there was scarcely anything to eat, where people lived crammed together in a single room, she succeeded with the scarcest of means in creating order and even a little, homey corner. She prepared tasty meals on a gas stove, which we shared with our friends. It was said: "Frau Schindler can conjure a roast goose from wood chips!"

In her last years, in Israel, she learned to bear her small, sad daily life in the tiny apartment in a way that was "well-behaved." But she bore it badly.

The Surviving Jews from Czernowitz

The Jews who survived Czernowitz scattered in all directions. They carried their heritage with them: the German-Jewish, bourgeois education; the sometimes contradictory values, habits of life, peculiarities and ways of expressing themselves; the German language they loved so much; the respect for Western culture; the love of books.

Many little local communities emerged, small groups in different exiles. They tried hard to sink roots in the new ground. Czernowitz's diversity, liveliness, and unease, its high expectations and hopes, gave strength and composure in many constellations, but in other cases proved to be a burden.

The encounter with the different cultures in the new homelands, and the demands that resulted, required the most varied kinds of assimilation. Thus, the past was reevaluated in ever new ways, crystallized into the most widely diverse images and memories, with different meanings.

I would say: Everyone who comes from there has his private, personal Czernowitz.

Czernowitz my black wit
with no foundation, that homeland
my homeland that taught me
to strike roots in the wind

pseudo-language
pseudo existence
masquerades
Purim games

driven here and there on the via dolorosa
Vienna – Paris – Przemysl

pseudo-nyms
phraso-nyms
megolomania
inadequacy

art
and a fall
high-flying leaps
Czernowitz my black wit.

from **Drafting a Life**

Leben im Entwurf

2012

Lasse die Deutung

Es glimmt der Ort wo Silben sich treffen

achte aufs Wort
der Sinn ist nicht einer

lasse die Deutung

begleite das Flüstern unter der Asche

* * *

Sie ruht nicht

ruht nicht seit langem
fragt wartet und horcht
wartet auf Antwort

im Dunkel
hinter dem Türspalt
erahnt sie ein Leuchten
Fasst sie's?
             Erfasst sie's?

* * *

Spreng

die Fessel der Schrift
lösch
das Geschriebne
finde Sprache

sprich sie
die von allen verstandene

Sprache

Leave interpretation

The place where syllables meet glows

attend to the word
its sense is not single

leave interpretation

go with the whispering under the ashes

* * *

She rests not

hasn't rested for a long time
asks waits and listens
waits for an answer

in the darkness
behind the crack under the door
she senses a shine
does she grasp it?

          Does she grasp its meaning?

* * *

Burst

the bonds of writing
erase
what's written
find speech

speak
what everyone understands

speech

Müde Metaphern

treiben
auf Trübwasserfläche
schweigen beredt
tauchen
nach dem Verborgensten
tauchen
nach Grund

* * *

Verse ungereimt

und zerstückt
treiben ihr Wesen
zwischen Zunge Gaumen
und Zähnen
vermarkten Vokabeln
verspielen das ICH und das DU

* * *

Fragmente

opak

so viel umsonst
so viel zuviel

so viel

Finger tasten sich vor
fügen zusammen
fügen zusammen

Tired metaphors

drift
on dirty water
in eloquent silence
dive for
what's most concealed
dive
for rock bottom

* * *

Verses, unrhymed

meaningless, cut to pieces
do what they do
between tongue palette
and teeth
hawk their morphemes
lose the I and the THOU

* * *

Fragments

opaque

so much in vain
so much too much

so much

fingers feel their way
put together
put together

Das gegängelte Hirn

speichert
abgewerkelte Texte
zerlesen
zerpflückt
zusammengeklebt

Collagen –

Collagen
        verstellen die Welt.

* * *

Wandernde Zeilen

zerlegen Sprache und Wort

zerlegen ein Leben
fehl am Ort
fehl an der Zeit

und doch
da steht eine Blume
Zeitlose im Frühling
        jäh blüht sie im Herbst

* * *

Mein

Wort-weg

fort-
weg

geht Neben-Wege

The stifled brain

stores
worked-over texts
read to pieces
picked to pieces
pasted together

collages –

collages
    deface the world.

      * * *

Wandering lines

parse language and word

parse a life
in the wrong place
at the wrong time

and yet
there's a flower
a springtime crocus
     suddenly blooms in autumn

      * * *

My

word-way

runs
off

goes sideways

Wortgefechte

morden mit
Worten
Sie reden mich an

zahllose Worte
die morden

kein Mahnmal
kein Name

* * *

Es war sehr spät

sie sprach zum ersten Mal
ihr endloses Gedicht

sie sprach zu sich

mit einer Stimme
die nicht ihre war
mit einer Zunge
die nicht ihre war

sprach
stockte

spricht
stockt
noch jetzt
mit einer Sprache die nicht meine ist
mit einer Zunge die nicht meine ist

Word battles

murder with
words
they speak to me

countless words
that murder

no monument
no name

* * *

It was very late

she spoke for the first time
her endless poem

she spoke to herself

in a voice
that was not hers
in a tongue
not hers

spoke
stammered

speaks
stammers
even now
in a language not mine
with a tongue not mine

Mattigkeit

mein Fastgedicht
mein Nochgedicht
muss Atem holen

es stösst an
meine Wahrheit
es stösst
an Sprache

ein Schattenspiel

* * *

Durch schwarze und weiße Felder geschoben

die Dame steht auf verlorenem Posten

König
und Läufer
verspielt

ein kleines Bäuerlein
hält Wache

matt

Weariness

my almost-poem
my already-poem
must take a breath

it collides with
my truth
it collides
with speech

a shadowplay

* * *

Moved across black and white fields

the queen holds a hopeless position

king
and bishop
forfeited

a little pawn
stands watch

mate

Nimm den Tag wie er kommt

Nimm den Tag

wie er kommt
leucht ihn aus

in deinem blauen Blick

wird keine Rose welken

* * *

Wenn nachts

die Geister zu mir kommen
finde ich Wahrheit
in der glattesten Lüge

morgens
die Geister verziehn sich
erspähe ich Lüge
in lauterster Wahrheit

* * *

Dieses Zugegensein der Abwesenden

der von uns Gegangenen

ihr Atemgang fremdet
in Vergänglichkeit

Take the day as it comes

Take the day

as it comes
shine a light on it

in your blue gaze

no rose shall wilt

* * *

At night when

ghosts come to me
I find truth
in the downright lie

next morning
the ghosts move on
I spy lies
in the purest truth

* * *

In mortality

their breathing sounds alien

the presence of those absent
of those who have left us

An der Grenze des Spätseins

kurz vor dem Zuspätsein
auf schmalster Plattform
erschafft sie
in Not
noch einmal
die eigenste
eine unmöglich Welt

* * *

Ein Baum

von Wünschen
entlaubt
vor dunklem Wasser-
spiegel

kahle Zweige
zeichnen
ein wellendes
Gesicht

* * *

Ohne Wollen

ohne Wünsche
erhebst du dich mühsam

Angst hinter dir
erblickst du im Spiegel
ein gebrochenes Bild

vertraue dem Sprung

On the border of lateness

almost too late
on the narrowest of platforms
needy
she creates
once more
her most private
impossible world

* * *

A tree

of wishes
leafless
against a dark mirror
of water

bare twigs
draw
a face
welling up

* * *

Without wanting

or wishes
you struggle to rise with difficulty

your fear behind you
in the mirror
you see a broken image

trust the leap

Festgeklammert

am Schrei
schwarzes Loch
im aufgerissenem Weiß

Schmerz
überbürdetes Wort
                reißt sich los

* * *

Geh in dein Herz-Minenfeld

wag es Schritt für Schritt zu durchkreuzen
grab den Wundacker um
Wortschollen kommen ins rollen
geh in dein Herz-Minen-Feld
lass es bersten
schaff dir neues Gelände

Clamped fast

to the scream
black hole
in the gaping white

pain
overburdened word
                escapes

                        * * *

Walk into your heart-minefield

dare to cross it, step by step
turn the wound-field over
word clods start into motion
go to your heart-minefield
let it explode
build your vacant land

59

Lass mich über Wiesen gehen

Tollen im Neuschnee

blendendes Weiß wie nie wieder
und wies frostig im Kindermund schmilzt

Flieder von damals
der Duft verborgener Veilchen
Gras frisch gemäht
glühende Sonne
träumen im Nussbaum
kleine grün-braune Finger
auf rauer Rinde

all das – darf man es nennen

es zieht

es zieht
die Hand meiner Schuester
die so früh wieder losließ

* * *

Democritus ridens Heraclitus flens

kein Spott mehr
kein Lamentieren

die Welt rollt wie je
schutzlos im All

die Menge steht bleiern

keiner tritt aus der Reihe
keiner sagt NEIN

Let me walk across meadows

Wrestling in fresh snow

blinding white as never again
and the way it melts in a child's mouth

lilacs from those days
the scent of hidden violets
fresh-mown grass
burning sunshine
dreams in the walnut tree
small green-brown fingers
on rough bark

all that – may we name it

it tugs

it tugs
at the hand of my sister
that let go so early

* * *

Democritus ridens Heraclitus flens

no more jeering
no laments

the world rolls on as always
defenseless in space

the leaden crowd stands

no one steps out of line
no one says NO

Demokrit lacht nicht mehr
Heraklit trockenen Auges
zuviel der Trauer
zuviel des Hohns
der Wahnsinn blindwütig wie je
es brennt die Leber vor Galle

die Menge klatscht töricht
an vorgeschriebenen Stellen

wer
       wagt
              was?

* * *

Gebet

Lass mich wieder Bäume sehn
lass mich über Weisen gehn
lass mich schauen mit Geduld
das kleine Flecken Grün
das uns noch blieb

lass mich noch einmal die Dinge
bei den rechten Namen nennen
mit Kinderworten

* * *

Landschaftlos

blicklos am Weg

bodenlos über das Field

baumlos im Wald

himmellos

der Mond

Gehen

Democritus has stopped laughing
Heraclitus is dry-eyed
too much mourning
too much scorn
madness rages
gall enflames the liver

the crows claps its foolish hands
where its told

who
        dares
                act?

* * *

Prayer

Let me see trees again
let me walk across meadows
let me patiently watch
the tiny green patch
left to us

let me call things once more
by the right names
with a child's words

* * *

Landscapeless

gazeless on the path

groundless over the field

in the woods treeless

skyless

the moon

Go

Verduckt

in der Uferlandschaft
trüb überspült

mein unnützes Ich
schluckt Tränen

furcht im Sand

* * *

Ein Mund

    zur Erde hingeneigt
nimmt den geknickten Halm
behutsam
    zwischen feuchte warme Lippen

er braucht
jeden Hauch

Hunched over

the shoreline
darkly washed

my useless I
swallows tears

furrows in sand

* * *

A mouth

      bowed down to earth
takes the bent blade
carefully
      between damp warm lips

it needs
every breath

Sand im Kopf

Lichthupen

Signale:
steh!
geh!

Warnzeichen
Sirenen

geh nicht! steh nicht!

halt dich bereit

Signale

* * *

Leben im Entwurf

    Lass das punktgenaue fragen
sag es zwischen hü und hott

    stottre stolpre zwischen Sätzen
lass die Fehler achtlos stehn

    wechsel Richtung je nach Laune
geh wohin's dich zieht

    nach Babel

* * *

Hick-hack:

es ist gar nicht so
es ist anders
und wiederum so
ganz anders
es ist wie es ist
es war immer schon so
    immer anders

Head full of sand

Signals

lights:
stop!
walk!

warning
sirens

don't walk! walk!

be prepared

signals

* * *

Drafting a life

    Stop your precise questioning
say it between giddy-up and whoa

    stutter stumble between statements
let the errors stand unheeded

    go wherever your mood may take you
let it pull you

    toward Babel

* * *

Hick-hack:

it is not at all like that
it is different
then again like that
completely different
it is how it is
it was always like that
    always different

Das Quäntchen Zeit

das ihr noch bleibt
spottwenig
unkalkulierbar

säumig verstiehlt sie's
das Quäntchen

* * *

Sand

im
Kopf
Kopf im Sand

Verwüstung

* * *

Treten am Laufband

du trittst weil du mußt

bleibst auf der Stecke

am Anfang
am Ende

am Anfang

The bit of time

that remains to her
ridiculously small
incalculable

tardily she steals it away
the bit

* * *

Sand

in the
head
head in the sand

desertification

* * *

Walking on the treadmill

you walk because you must

give up halfway

at the start
at the end

at the start

Stunden des Möchtegenies

im Bett vor dem Aufstehn
wie Jesus die Welt umarmen
dichten wie Hölderlin

mit halbgeschlossen Augen
wie ein Kind Schokolade kauen

unbehaglich das Schauen
in der Früh
aus dem Fenster

* * *

Inserat

Selbstalut
selbstisch und selbstwund
sucht selbstlosen Mitlaut zum Mitlauf:
konsonant

Hours of a would-be genius

In bed before rising
embrace the world like Jesus
write poems like Hölderlin

with half-closed eyes
eat chocolate like a child

first thing
out the window
the view is unsettling

* * *

Advertisement

Vowel
own one's own wound
seeks selfless consonant
for consonance

Ohne Boden war die Heimat

Czernowitz mein schwarzer Witz:
Ohne Boden war die Heimat
meine Heimat die mich schulte
Wurzeln in den Wind zu schlagen

Pseudo-Sprache
Pseudo-Dasein
Maskeraden
Purimspiele

umgetrieben auf dem Kreuzweg
Wien – Paris – Przemysl

Pseudo-nyme
Phraseo-nyme
Grössenwahn und
Ungenügen

Kunst
und Sturz
und Höhenflüge
Czernowitz mein schwarzer Witz

* * *

In die scharfen Zacken des Judensterns
verbissen

die Zunge wundgeschnitten

ein Schluck bitteren Wassers
aus totem Meer

Homeland with no foundation

Cernowitz my black wit
with no foundation, that homeland
my homeland that taught me
to strike roots in the wind

pseudo-language
pseudo-existence
masquerades
Purim games

driven here and there on the via dolorosa
Vienna – Paris – Przemysl

pseudo-nyms
phraso-nyms
megolomania
inadequacy

art
and a fall
high-flying leaps
Cernowitz my black wit

* * *

On the points of the Jewish star
hard bitten

tongue cut open

a swallow of bitter water
from a dead sea

Post Holocaust – kaustisch

post holokaustisch zelebriert
post-festum es tut kaum noch weh
holo-holo ganz feierlich
wird um die Asche mnemisiert

es qualmt es brennt
post-prä
        paßt auf

          * * *

Es gibt nichts heileres auf der Welt
als ein gebrochenes jüdisches Herz
– Rabbi Nachman von Bratzlaw

Ein jüdisches Herz ist nicht heil

bricht nicht

hoffnungslos hofft es
verhofft sich
verharzt
und
verherzt

          * * *

Bangen um's Land

wo so schnell gesiegt wird –
gesiegt und verloren
gebaut und zerstört
gepflanzt und vertilgt

es gibt keine Zeit für das Leid
Hierzulande
wo Gott gelobt wird
bigott

74

Post-Holocaust – caustic

post-Holocaustically celebrated
post festum it hardly hurts anymore
holo-holo, solemnly
the ashes are mnemitized

it smokes, it burns
post-pre
                    looks sharp

                    * * *

> There is nothing more whole in the world
> than a broken Jewish heart
> – Rabbi Nachman of Bratslav

A Jewish heart is not whole

does not break

hopelessly, it hopes itself
to pieces
is gummed
and hearted
to pieces

                    * * *

Worry about the country

where victory comes so fast –
won and lost
built and destroyed
planted and plowed under

there is no time for suffering
in this homeland
where God is praised
with bigotry

Feste des Friedens

elektronisch gesteuert
lautstark orchestriert

sie hissen die Fahnen und hassen
in der Arena wird Frieden gedroht

er jagt durch die Neblung
Landschaft entzieht sich
kein Osten kein Westen

kein Horizont

Peace celebrations

electronically managed
harsh orchestration

in the arena they threaten peace
hoist flags and hate

it flees through fog
landscape vanishes
no East no West

no horizon

Mein Kennwort in dir

Du kommst zurück

greifst nach den Scherben
hebst Licht aus Tempeltiefen
schreitest auf Königswegen
durch vermauerte Tore

ist's Tod ist's Verheißung?

* * *

Zeichen

vom Messer gezogen
queren Stirn und Brust

        er schreit
        seinen Psalm
        von der Brücke

        "Ich geh". . .

* * *

Du hast dich immer gegen mich gewehrt

war's Wahrheit war es Lüge?

Und ich? – auch ich hab mich gewehrt
      war's Wahrheit war es Lüge?

Jetzt fast nach Schluß
      Lass uns gewähren!

My code word in you

You come back

try to grasp the shard
lift light from temples' depths
stride down King's roads
through bricked-over doors

is it death, or the Promised Land?

* * *

Signs

drawn by a knife
crisscross temples and breast

        he shouts
        his psalm
        from the bridge

        "I am going"...

* * *

You always resisted me

was it truth, was it a lie?

And I? – I too resisted
        was it truth, was it a lie?

Now almost past the end
        Let us be!

Was will ich von dir

ich will wissen was gilt
mein Kennwort erkennen in dir

und meine Not

* * *

Sag:

haben wir uns je gekannt
je zu erkennen gegeben
uns wahrgenommen
gehalten, gegeben

Sag "es ist schön"

einmal war's schön
wahr
        schön

What I want from you

I want to know what holds true
to recognize my code word in you

and my need

                         * * *

Say:

have we ever known each other
made signs of recognition
perceived each other
held, given

say "It is beautiful."

once it was beautiful
truly
                    beautiful

from **Between Now and Now**

Zwischen dem Jetzt und dem Jetzt

2007

Stehen am Kreuzweg

Sags
Sag es anders
lern deine Zeit neu bemessen
lern wieder zu träumen im Schlaf
lerne erwachen

mit Fäden aus Zwielicht
web dir von neuem
Stirne und Augen
und Mund

* * *

Beredt
im Vorgedanklichen
steckend
kasper ich
tief – tief
im Unterholz

dichternd

* * *

Genialisch schief ists gegangen
zuviel und zuwenig verstanden
fest festgefahren
in rosafarbenen Kinderstuben
im Kitsch der kleinen Ästhetik

Standing at the crossing

Say it
Say it otherwise
learn to take a new measure of time
to put dreams back in your sleep
to wake up

with threads of twilight
weave new
forehead eyes
mouth

* * *

Eloquently
stuck
in half thoughts
I jerk like a puppet
deep – deep
in the underbrush

poeticizing

* * *

A genius at failure
having understood too much and too little
solidly stuck
in a rosy-hued childhood
in the kitsch of a small aesthetics

du mußt fort
es ist spät

du fragst
nach der Richtung

"Gib auf, gibs auf!"

                     kichert K's Schutzmann

* * *

Im Zug von Basel nach Düsseldorf

In meiner Fensterecke
besing ich dich
Schönheit des Rheins

in Köln das Schild:
Umschlagbahnhof
Umschlagplatz raunt es…

Schönheit des Rheins

* * *

Mein Puls schlägt Widerhaken
paroxysmal

der Morgen schikaniert bereits
mit neuen Streichen

von den Kathedern
wird Untergang doziert

you must go
it is late

you ask
for directions

"Give up, give up!"
                    K's policeman smirks

                    * * *

In the train from Basel to Düsseldorf

From my seat at the window
I sing of you
beauty of the Rhine

In Cologne the memorial plaque:
transfer station
whispers *deportation…*

O beauty of the Rhine

                    * * *

My pulse beats against the grain
paroxysmal

this morning is already playing
new tricks

from the pulpits they preach
destruction

Phantomschmerz

Fortamputiertes
lahmt durch den Raum

der entlaubte Leib
            bäumt sich im Widerwort auf

* * *

Lasse mich sprechen

die Erste werd ich nicht sein
und nicht die Letzte

doch lass mich
lasse mich sprechen

            ohne Meister

* * *

Du sprichst vom lichtscheuen Held
    des Nichtgetanhabens
du sprichst vom dauernden Rennen
    auf ausgetretenen Pfaden
vom Stehen am Kreuzweg

du sprichst…

denke:
es geht
um das fiebrige
Vielleichtdoch

Phantom pain

Amputated limbs
limp through space

the bare trunk
          writhes in the anti-word

             * * *

Let me speak

I will not be the first
nor last

only allow me
allow me to speak

         with no master

            * * *

You speak of the unsung hero
    of things not done
you talk of constantly running
    down beaten paths
of standing at the crossing

you speak…

think:
what matters
is the fevered
"but maybe"

Irgendwann geschiehts
etwas in mir
man könnte es Liebe nennen
verkümmert

ich höre wie es stirbt in mir
beharrlich
ohne Metapher

* * *

Wunde wird Wort
Wort wird Gebärde
Gebärde Gedicht

mein Ja im Nein

* * *

meine Länder
meine Lieben
meine Lieder
ortlos

* * *

Aufschrei:
Schriftkeil aus der Verstörung

gegen die Sprachwand

At some point it happens
something in me
you could call it love
shrinks away

I hear it dying in me
insistent
without metaphor

* * *

Wound becomes word
word becomes gesture
gesture a poem

my Yes in the No

* * *

My lands

my loves

my songs

without a place

* * *

A cry:
cuneiform dart of confusion

against the wall of language

In spärlicher Wortlandschaft
sprachgestört
fahrig
setz ich das lästige Leid
doch noch
in Versfüße um

In a landscape nearly bereft of words
language disturbed
wavering
I set troublesome suffering
in verse
after all

Im Stundenglas

Zwischen dem Jetzt und dem Jetzt

unüberbrückbar

im Nu ists vorbei
nie wieder wie früher
nie wieder wie jetzt

der Zeiger verrückt

an die Rädchen geklammert
synchronisiert
die Schließmundschnecke

kleine Klausilie

* * *

Im Stundenglas rieselts

es schlägt keine Stunde

die Stunde steht Kopf

mein kleiner Planet
rollt schwerlos im All
kein Oben
kein Unten
schmal schimmert die Aura
im Schwarz

In the hourglass

Between now and now

unbridgeable

it is gone in a flash
never again the way it was
never again the way it is

the minute hand ticks

grasps the cogs
synchronizes
the shut-your-mouth spring

small subordinate clause

* * *

The hourglass trickles

no hour chimes

the hour does a headstand

my small planet
rolls weightless through space
no up
no down
its small aura
shimmers in the dark

Tief in der runden Stunde meiner Nacht
im Schoß der Dunkelheit
hör ichs im Gleichmaß atmen

ich warte
dass die Unruh von mir geht
dann kreis ich langsam
           auf die andre Seite meiner Zeit

                    ich sehe die Konturen
      von dem was drüben drängt

      und bete für die stille Umsicht dieser Stunde
im Schoß der Dunkelheit

* * *

Sedimente

Grau-Gestein
Schwarz-Gestein
und auch Buntes

gestaffelt
fest ineinandergefügt

zwing dich hinein
schaff Platz für die Träne

* * *

Ein Mal
mein Mal
brech ich den Bann

leg meinen Finger aufs Wundmal
ein Mal
* * *

Zeuge
für deinen Tag

Deep in the rounded hour of my night
in the womb of darkness
even breathing is heard

I wait
for the restlessness to leave me
then I slowly turn over
                    to the other side of my time

                              I see the contours
         of what presses urgently from there

         and pray for the quiet consideration of this hour
in the womb of darkness

* * *

Sediments

Gray stone
black stone
bright stone

stacked up
fit snug

force your way in
make room for tears

* * *

Wound, once
my once-wound
I break the spell

touch my finger to the wound
wound-once
                              * * *

Witness
for your day

leuchte ihn aus
schaffe ihm Dauer

denk dran –

        Jemand geht mit

              * * *

Steilabfall
greif dir noch schnell
den Stein
          im Geröll
den mit den Adern durchwachsenen
den Arterit

du kannst baun

              * * *

Lass dein Herz nicht zu laut werden wenn
das zu Gedenkende –
das zu Vergessende –
täglich neu auf dich zukommt

du scheust zurück

du wolltest springen

              * * *

Ich wollte eine Werkstatt bauen
für krauses Denken

ich wollte Ackerstrecken ziehen
und Lust dran haben

den Fremden wollte ich zum Tanze laden
die Hände der Geschwister halten

ich wollte…
Zauderin hinter beschlagenem Glas

so habe ich mich nicht gewollt

shine a light on it
give it duration

think of it –

          Someone goes with you

               * * *

Steep slope
quick, grasp
the stone
         in the moraine
the one with veins growing through it
the arterite

you can build
             * * *

Don't let your heart beat too loud when
what you ought to remember –
what you ought to forget –
comes at you day after day

you start back

you wanted to leap

             * * *

I wanted to build a workshop
for muddled thinking

I wanted to set out furrows
rejoice in them

I wanted to invite the stranger to dance,
hold hands with sisters

I wanted…
hesitating behind a fogged-over glass

I did not want to be like this

Und die verwaisten Hände

Auch ich hab deine Gesänge verwirkt
Schotter unter der Zunge
stotter ich
hin
zum Mandelstab
den du mir gabst

mit ihm
der nächste Schritt

* * *

Du sahst mich an
da wußt ichs
es ist mein Gesicht
längst schon abhanden

dein Blick und mein Gesicht in deinem Blick

abhanden –

und die verwaisten Hände

* * *

Sie stapft durch den Zeitstaub
mühselig

rät die Pfade
die sie nicht kennt

der Tote schreitet voran

leicht geht er
und aufrecht

sie hinkt hinterher
der Wahnscherben scheppert

"Es lebe der König"

And the orphaned hands

I too have incurred your songs
gravel under my tongue
I stutter
on
toward the almond branch
that you gave me

with it
the next step

* * *

You looked at me
and I knew
my face is
long gone, unhanded

your gaze and my face in your gaze

long gone –

and the orphaned hands

* * *

She wades through time's dust
with difficulty

guesses the paths
she does not know

the deceased precedes her

strides lightly
and upright

she follows limping
shards of madness clatter

"Long live the king"

Was zu dir stand an
jedem der Ufer,
es tritt gemäht in ein anderes Bild
— Paul Celan

Jahre danach
wieder das Leuchten
"der Eisvogel taucht
es sirrt die Sekunde"

beim Eukalyptus
am Jordan
steh ich
steh im Bild –

      ungemäht

von hier fließ ich mit:
fließ mit dem Pruth
fließ mit der Oka
fließ mit der Seine

* * *

Fortgetan von hastigen Händen
in Thiais Paris Orly
der Jud
der Dichter

      – nicht davongekommen –

Tiefflug
von Ost und von West
kreuzt sich
im Himmel, im Abgrund

überm Granitblock
flattert es deutsch

kein Halm
kein Stein
kein Weiß
nichts "Großgeweintes"

What stood toward you
on each of the banks,
it steps mown down into a different image
– Paul Celan

Years later
again the glow
"the kingfisher dives
the second whirrs"

by the eucalyptus
on Jordan's banks
I stand
in the image, stand –
                    unmown

from here I flow too:
flow with the Pruth
flow with the Oka
flow with the Seine

* * *

Buried with hasty hands
in Thiais Paris Orly
the Jew
the poet
                    – he did not escape –

low-flying planes
from east and west
crisscross
the heavens, the abyss

on the granite block
something German flutters

no blade of grass
no stone
no whiteness
nothing "wept large"

Der Kreis den du gezogen
gilt er?
gilt er nicht?

wie damals gebannt
im Wahn des Erkennens
spiel ich mit den Scherben

verbannt
kahlgeschoren

* * *

Wir
wissen ja nicht,
was
gilt
— Paul Celan

Der Sprung im Krug
"gilt"
es strahlt im tönernen
Innern.

Das Leuchten
"gilt"

* * *

Mehr als dein Blick
       dein Wort und deine Hand
hat mich dein Schmerz erkannt
Narbe um Narbe befühlt
Wunde um Wunde geprüft

über dem Ich
über dem Du

The circle you drew
does it hold true?
does it not hold true?

spellbound, as then,
in the delusion of knowing
I play with the shards

exiled
with my shaved head

* * *

We
don't know
what
holds true
– Paul Celan

The crack in the jug
"holds true"
something shines through the clay
within

the glow
"holds true"

* * *

More than your gaze
            your word and your hand
your pain knew me
felt scar after scar
tested wound after wound

above the I
above the you

Der "Königsweg" ist nicht meiner
ich bieg um die Ecke

die erträumte Heimat
hat bankrottiert
blieb ein kleines Zuhaus
ohne Garten und Blick

ich bieg um die Ecke
gehe dem nach
was nicht ruhn läßt

* * *

Unter Basalt und trockenen Kränzen

er wartet nicht –

doch sie kommen
sie kommen in Scharen
die gar Gelahrten
kommen und graben
"Helfenichtse" von eh –
und die Neuen –
stehlen die Silbermünze von der Zunge
prägen sie neu

er stört nicht

zuweilen aber spukt er
mutwillig
in manchen Köpfen
                  und Seelen
stiftet Unheil…

The "King's Road" is not mine
I corner

the *Heimat* we dreamed of
is bankrupt
what's left – a few rooms
without garden or view

I corner
pursue what
won't let me rest

                    * * *

Under basalt and dry wreaths

he does not wait –

still they come
in their legions
the oh-so educated
come and they dig
the old "help-me-nots"
and the new ones –
steal the silver coin from the tongue
coin it new

he does not resist

but his mischievous ghost
flits at times
through some heads
                    and souls
makes trouble…

Novembersonne tastet mich aus
hier am Berg überm See
Genezareth
Herbst –
Zeitlose
am Felsrand
blaß
vor dem starken Blau eines Himmels

im Galil
duften die trockenen Gräser herb

ich bins
die da atmet
und schaut
Zeitloses
über dem Wasser

* * *

Meine Zunge haftet am Gaum
wenn ich deiner gedenke
Jerusalem

in Freude kam ich zu dir
ich stand im Licht
und um mich standen die Tore

immer gedenke ich deiner
dräng mich an das Vermauerte

wo ist dein Zauber?

du haftest am Gaum
bitter und hart

November sun fingers me over
here, overlooking the sea
Nazareth
autumn crocus
pale
at cliff's edge
against
the strong blue of a heaven

Galilee's
strong grasses acrid smell

it is I
who breathe
see
timelessness bloom
over the water

* * *

My tongue sticks to my palette
as I think of you
Jerusalem

I came to you joyfully
stood in the light
and the gates stood around me

I hold you in memory
thrust against what's walled in

where is your magic?

you stick to my palette
bitter and hard

Den Ölberg hinab
schleppt den Teufelsfuß
hinter sich her
verschleppt sich das Urteil

die Wildsau zertrampelt
was einmal gekeimt

der stete Hahnenschrei
aus jener Herrgottsfrühe
kann die Wahrheit nicht steigern

Dominus flevit

* * *

Geh in die Wüste Hoseas

LO RUCHAMA
dir wird Erbarmen nicht

Nichtvolk
Nichtweib des Nichtmanns
Nichtkind des Nichtgotts
Nicht beim Namen gedacht

kehre um in die Rede Hoseas
ohne Bogen und Schwert
wird Erbarmen
zuteil.

Down the Mount of Olives
judgment drags
the devil's foot
after it

the wild boar tramples
what budded there

the constant cock's crowing
from the crack of that dawn
can't make truth more true

Dominus flevit

* * *

Go to Hosea's desert

LO RUCHAMA
no mercy awaits you

non-people
non-wife of non-husband
non-child of non-god
not recalled by name

turn back to the word of Hosea
lay down the bow and the sword
mercy
will be yours

Du rührst ans Lied

Ich hab Leben gewählt
mit dem ganzen Ballast
die Füße sind schwer
und es versagt
mir die Stimme

ich gehe leicht durch den Spiegel

Sicht wird frei

* * *

Wenn morgens die Uhr schlägt
schlägst du die Augen nicht auf
kapitulierst nicht

im alten Hinterzimmer
legst du dir täglich den Text aus

* * *

Wem es das Wort nie
verschlagen hat
— Ingeborg Bachmann

Die, der es die Worte verschlägt
kehrt auf halbem Weg um

die, die ihren Namen nicht kennt
kann nicht unterschreiben

stammelt unhaltbare Sätze
zwischen Vorsatz und Vorsatz

Touch the song

I have chosen life
with all its ballast
the feet are heavy
and my voice
fails

lightly I cross over the mirror

sight is set free

* * *

When the clock strikes morning
you don't open your eyes
don't capitulate

in the old back room
you decipher the daily text

* * *

Who was never
left speechless
– Ingeborg Bachmann

She who is left speechless
turns back halfway

she who does not know her name
cannot sign it

stammers untenable sentences
from intent to intent

113

Die, die nur halbspricht
spricht zuviel
verspricht sich
spricht weiter
spricht nie aus
zerspricht

* * *

In Wortfächern kramen
ein Zauberwort turnt
links-rechts
im Gehirn

Fragwürdiges
schichtet sich um

scharf zugespitzt mündet
der Bleistift

* * *

Wachschlaf
nie durchstandener Alp

entkommen
zum Traum hin
zum Lilienohr hin

in lautlosem Flug
ohne Halt

* * *

Geballter Zeitrest
hüpft provokant
Zick-Zack
den Weg voran
grimmig jage ich nach

ich muss eine Schuld begleichen

She who only half speaks
speaks too much
misspeaks
goes on speaking
never speaks all
speaks it to pieces

* * *

Cramming in word drawers
a magic word tumbles
left-right
in the brain

re-layers
things questioned

sharp-pointed, the pencil
mouths

* * *

Waking sleep
unfinished nightmare

escaped
toward the dream
toward the lily's ear

in soundless flight
with nothing to hold onto

* * *

Dense time's remainder
hops provocatively
zigzag
on the path
grimly, I run after it

I must square an account

Pausenlos laufen
auf ebener Windung

die Mitte rückt weiter

gerät außer Sicht

* * *

Ich schicke meine Rede aus
doch sie macht kehrt

klein
hart
geballt
holt sie zum Schlag aus

* * *

Komm
spiel mit dir allein
Himmel und Hölle

Spiel wie das Kind mit dem Stein

hüpf über den Strich –
ohne Angst
vor der Angst

* * *

Erträgst du nur
den nächsten Augenblick
des bloßen Seins
erfindest dir dein Ja
hältst ein

lotest dein Dunkel aus
rührst an das Lied

To run without stopping
on an even curve

the center moves off

is lost to sight

* * *

I send forth my talk
but it turns back

small
hard
a fist
it gets ready to punch

* * *

Come
play alone
hopscotch between heaven and hell

Play like the child with the stone

hop over the line –
with no fear
of fear

* * *

Only endure
the next moment
of naked existence
you'll invent your Yes
call a halt

plumb your darkness
touch the song

117

Ich vermess das Gefälle
suche es ab

klaub Hoffnungssplitter zusammen

staffel sie
fächer sie auf

staffel sie
fächer sie auf

* * *

Die Nacht
sie droht mir nicht

es ist gut
es ist Nacht
es ist still

die Toten und die Sterbenden sind nah –
wir wissen voneinander –
wir sind wahr
vergeben Sünden

mir droht der Tag

* * *

Hier ist das Buch
hier ist der Stab
er weist den Weg
durchs Blättergewühl
führt in den Spätherbst
da soll ich beginnen
wo einmal die Schule begann
die ich verschlief
da soll ich beginnen
mit dem Buch
mit dem Stab

I measure the slope
explore it

grab splinters of hope

stack them
lay them out

stack them
lay them out

* * *

The night
does not threaten me

it is good
it is night
it is still

the dead and the dying are close –
we know of each other –
we are true
forgive sins

day threatens me

* * *

Here is the book
here is the rod
it points the way
through the surging leaves
leads to late fall
where I should begin
where the school once began
that I slept through
where I should begin
with the book
with the rod

Nie wieder laufen gegen den Wind

Der Geigerzähler tickt
ein Halm nach dem andern
knickt im sauren Regen

nie wieder laufen
gegen den Wind

Vergiß nicht vom moosigen Stein zu träumen
seit tausend Jahren liegt er im Bergbach

* * *

Die Spanne
          Spannung
Drehung im Tanz:
Wendung
herbeigewünscht
verwünscht

Anti-Strophe

Schlußakt
          Befreiung.

* * *

Im Schüttstein des Seins
zähl ich die Schrammen
zähle – zähl nach
es geht nicht auf

Zuflucht am Ort
wo der Stein bricht.

Never again to run against the wind

The Geiger counter ticks
one blade, then another
is bent by the acid rain

never again to run
against the wind

Don't forget to dream of the mossy stone
it has lain in the mountain brook for a thousand years

* * *

Tensed time
                tension
a turn in the dance:
the wished-for
the much-maligned
turn

anti-strophe

final act
                freedom

* * *

In the sewer of being
I count the scrapes
count – recount
it does not add up

refuge in the place
where the stone breaks

Wär ich auch in Arkadien geboren
es gäbe Tränen
                im Spätherbst

Schönheit
wird
        Last

* * *

Wen der Pfeil des Schönen je getroffen
Ewig währt für ihn der Schmerz der Liebe
                                — August von Platen

Der Pfeil des Schönen
hat mich nicht
getroffen
hat mich
gestreift
er reißt
am unsichtbaren
Wundmal

* * *

Reizbar – vor Schönheit
zornig – den Menschen
unwillig – der Natur
Liebes-
        Unverstand
Liebe
        unaustauschbar

un
aus
tauschbar?

Had I been born in Arcadia
there would still be tears
                    in the late fall

beauty
becomes
            hard to bear

                            * * *

                            For him who is struck by beauty's arrow
                                the pain of love endures forever
                                    – August von Platen

The arrow of beauty
did not
strike me
glanced
off me
tears
at the unseen
wound

                            * * *

Sensitive – to beauty
angry – at mankind
stubborn – by nature
love
            un-understood
love
            inexchangeable

in
ex
changeable?

Mit deinem Schmerz – mein Kind –
hab ich zu wenig gelitten
meine Hand hat zu leicht
auf deinem Scheitel geruht
unsre Wege zu eng
um nebeneinander zu gehen

gib deinen Schmerz frei
es geht um Abschied
es geht um Leben

* * *

Und wenn die Klage ausklingt
bleibt dann noch
eine Ahnung von Gott?
und ein Kind?
ein fragender Blick zum Menschen
der vor dir steht?
und der Rest deines Atems
für Etwas das grün ist
und duftet?

* * *

Auch dieses Jahr kommt die Frau
in den Garten
ihre Gießkanne leck

hochgestreckt steht sie
ein drohender Finger
auf geborstener Erde

steht und wartet

I suffered too little – my child –
with your pain
my hand rested too lightly
on the crown of your head
our paths were too close
to walk side by side

set your pain free
it is about good-bye
it is about life

* * *

And when the dirge ends
does there remain
some vague sense of God?
and a child?
a questioning gaze at the person
who stands before you?
and the rest of your breath
for something green
and fragrant?

* * *

This year as well, the woman
comes to the garden
with her leaky watering can

drawn up tall
a threatening finger
on cracked earth

she stands and waits

sie wartet im Grasland
sie wartet im Sand
sie wartet im Schlamm
die Ebbe wartet sie ab
und die Flut
und die länger werdenden Schatten.

Sie wartet am Weltrand

* * *

Sieben Jahrzehnte
sterb ich mein Leben

Wüste jagt hinter mir her
holt mich ein
ich zähle die Dünen
sieben mal zehn

Kopf im Sand

* * *

Reden von Toten
Unmitteilbares
auf unkluger Zunge

wir rufen sie wach

wir zwingen sie mitzuleben
in unserer Welt
umklammert von Worten
uns zum Trost

es friert

waits in the grassland
waits in the sand
waits in the mud
waits for the ebb
and the flood tide
the lengthening shadows

she waits at the edge of the world

* * *

For seven decades
I have died my life

desert pursues me
catches up with me
I count the dunes
seven times ten

my head in the sand

* * *

Talk of the dead –
unmediated
on incautious tongues

we waken them with our call

we force them to live with us
in our world
held fast by our words
for our own comfort

it is freezing

Neige dich zu deinen Toten
sie hören
sie schauen
sie leben dir zu

sprechen dir zu
kaum noch vernehmbar

weißt du noch?

* * *

Aug in Aug mit dem Gestern
Aug in Aug mit dem Jetzt

ein Leben

Staubkorn unter der Lupe
Geschichte in die Pupille gebrannt
zerstört Lichtsinnzellen

* * *

Käme doch einer und fragte genau
nach dem Was und dem Wie und dem
Muss-es-so-sein?

Käme doch einer
bestünde auf Antwort

gäbe acht
auf das Was und das Wie

Ich weiß
ich täte was sein muss

Bow down to your dead
they hear
they are watching
they live toward you

speak toward you
barely perceptible

do you remember?

* * *

Eye to eye with yesterday
eye to eye with the now

a life

a dust mote under the magnifier
history branded onto the pupil
destroys light-sensitive cells

* * *

If someone came and asked me precisely
about the what and the how and the
must-it-be-like-this?

If someone came
and insisted on an answer

paid attention
to the what and the how

I know
I would do what needs to be done

Horch und schau
es ist möglich

das Licht leuchtet neu
die Melodie erklingt wieder
ein Kinderspruch gilt noch:
Müde bin ich geh zur Ruh
schließe meine Augen zu …
Vater –

ich rede dich an

Listen well and look
it is possible

the light shines anew
the melody sounds again
a childish saying is still true:
now I lay me down to sleep
close my eyes before I do...
Father –

I speak to you

Schriftkeile

Schriftkeile
auf pergamentener
Haut

das Gesicht
gezeichnet
bis auf die Knochen

* * *

Ein Antlitz
bloßgelegt

aus benetzten Lidspalten
gehn Sehkeime auf

* * *

Wüstengeschiebe

Sandwege
durch-fahnden

Dünengras-Flüstern
im Mund-Ohr:

finden

Cuneiform

Cuneiform
on parchment
skin

the face
marked
to the bone

* * *

A countenance
laid bare

from dampened slits
seeds of sight germinate

* * *

Desert moraine

search through
sand paths

dune grass whispers
in the mouth-ear:

find

Kein Platz für Gräber
in der Herzkammer
zerscherben
Urnen

ruhlose Finger
kneten Gebete
aus gebrannter Erde
aus Ton

* * *

Im Flachflug
nach Singendem greifen
segeln

ohne Orient

* * *

Lasst mich
Zwingt mir die Ordnung nicht auf
mühet mich nicht mit der Ratio

im Widersinn
finde ich Zuflucht

* * *

Wieder Bäume sehn
über Wiesen gehn
den schmalen Streifen
Gras befühlen

Atem holen
die Dinge
bei den ersten Namen nennen

No place for graves
in the heart's chamber
urns
shard

restless fingers
knead prayers
from scorched earth
of clay

* * *

In low flight
try to grasp singing
sail

with no Orient

* * *

Leave me alone
don't annoy me with reason
impel me to order

in non-sense
I find refuge

* * *

To see trees again
walk across meadows
feel the narrow
strip of grass

Take a breath
call things
by first names

Auf Leben und Tod
gestammelt

das leere Blatt
wehrt ab

* * *

Wortströme
Hörströme
Gleichzeitigkeiten
Zungenvielfalt
Splittersprache

steigen aus dem Gerede
kunstlos
gerade

* * *

Du stehst am Ort
wo
Silben
sich treffen

achte aufs Wort
        auf den Bruch

es flüstert
unter der Asche

Vom Waisenwort her
wo die Unrast begann

von da muss ich Leben entwerfen
für Antwort einstehn

Stammered at risk
of life and death

the blank page
refuses

* * *

Word streams
hearing streams
simultaneities
multiple tongues
splinter-language

rise up from mere talk
artlessly
straight

* * *

You stand at the place
where
syllables
meet

attend to the word
        to the break

there are whispers
under the ashes

From the orphan word
where the unease began

from there, drafting a life
stands for answers

A Conversation Between Norman Manea and Ilana Shmueli

Jerusalem, December 2009

Norman Manea: How changed was he? I don't mean only with respect to his age.

Ilana Shmueli: My first meeting with Paul after the war was in Paris.

NM: When was this?

IS: Before the Six-Day War, I believe, in Fall '65, I traveled to Paris. I had already been to Europe several times, but this was my first visit to Paris. Celan's address and telephone number were given to me by a mutual friend. Celan's number was a secret. The first evening I walked around Paris alone. It was late summer. I looked him up, but no one was at home, and I left a message with my phone number and the address of my hotel on his door. Then we met, for the first time in twenty-one years. Indeed I found him very changed—somewhat carelessly dressed and much heavier than I remembered him. He approached me openly and with joy. He was, at the time, about fifty, and I was forty-five.

NM: No longer very young.

IS: No longer very young. Yet it was a good reunion, which then became a bit complicated, since both of us, after all, were complicated. (We already knew this from our time in Czernowitz.) The initial sense of estrangement rapidly resolved, and almost from the first moment we found our common language. Everything went smoothly, and we had a lot to tell each other. We met in the late afternoon and walked all night through the streets of Paris. He suggested that I make secret wishes on coins and toss them into the Seine from the Pont Neuf. Early in the morning, we arrived at Les Halles. Celan bought me a bundle of radishes instead of flowers and we were happy. Then naturally we ate onion soup—which of course belonged to his time in Paris.

NM: And your meeting in Jerusalem?

IS: That was about three years later. In Paris, when we parted I had promised him that if he were to come to Israel I would be his "guide" in Jerusalem, as wonderful a guide as he had been for me on this night in Paris. After this meeting, we wrote several letters to each other. And after his death his wife found an unsent letter from this time, which she gave to me, along with all my own letters. In that letter he informs me of a possible visit to Jerusalem.

NM: As I told you before, I was very impressed by these letters, I even had the feeling they should be similar to Milena's (lost) letters to Kafka. This very deep connection—how to describe it?—a dialogue that was no dialogue and yet was more than a dialogue. What they say, what don't say, and how that dialogue is understood by both correspondents is deeply moving.

IS: For me he was not really so difficult to understand. I think we were very close; there were many similarities between us. Although externally I mostly behaved as one who fit in. I did not feel free to live and act out my own peculiarly individual personality traits, as I would have liked to do, and as he mostly did.

NM: Yes, I understand.

IS: Very often he seized the right to behave according to his moods, and these were not always very congenial and not always pleasant. Already in Czernowitz, in the ghetto, we discovered that in our emotional world we had a lot in common—volatility, ambiguity, hypersensitivity, contradictoriness. He found me "cheeky" (which I was, too) and overly critical. Later, when I read his letters and poems, I often had the feeling that I, myself, would have to write this. I felt it as a part of me—now, I know, this is presumptuous. I discovered something strange in these last days. I am now working on a short afterword for the little volume, *Say that Jerusalem Is.* My publisher wants to release a new edition. Going through the little book I found the poem:

> *Einen Stiefel voll Hirn*
> *in den Regen gestellt.*
> *Es wird ein Gehn sein, ein großes*
> *weit über die Grenzen,*
> *die uns ziehn.*

It struck me that I had recorded "Gehn sein" as *one single* word in the epilogue. As a stopping, a halting, a self-continuing state of being, thus *ein großes Gehnsein*, "a great goingbeing." It was a neologism, which to me seemed very natural for Celan. Especially these poems—whose contexts I knew and whose creation I had been present for—seemed very close to me.

NM: Were you prepared at that moment to give shelter to such a soul as he was? Was this an expectation; was this also perhaps a wish, a desire to receive—shall we say—such a complicated yet brotherly soul?

IS: Ever since our time in Czernowitz he has remained alive in me. There we were part of a group that came together to read and discuss things with one another, but Paul was for me—and not only for me— the center. Then what came simply came.

NM: I suspect in Paris he was not the same person as in Czernowitz. Was there a great change? And was there an expectation?

IS: Apparently there were some sorts of expectations, representations had been made. A mutual friend (still from the time in the ghetto) came at that time from Paris and told me a lot about him. He brought me a handwritten copy of "*Todesfuge*" and also a copy of "The Meridian." I understood little at the time. Yet as I read "The Meridian" over again following our meetings and conversations, it grew different. I also desired and anticipated these conversations. His texts spoke to me very directly, even if I often did not wholly comprehend them.

NM: Of course in his case there was a code, and step by step one had to learn to break the code in order to understand it.

IS: Yes, there were also codes that were entirely our own. When he began to send me the poems, those he said he had written for me, I had the feeling of intimacy—of knowledge. I, too, had experienced, had been present when they arose, in their creation. When I was in Paris, he read aloud for me his last two books, already prepared for publication, *Lichtzwang* [*Lightduress*] and *Schneepart* [*Snowpart*]. He read me each of these books twice in succession, one after the other, the whole book, without interruption. And I asked nothing, not a thing. Nor did I have any need to ask questions, although I knew that this would be a fantastic opportunity to talk about his poetry. He would rarely speak about his poems, and I knew this. He wanted to read and read.

NM: He did not want to explain himself.

IS: He did not want to explain himself, but for example, the first poem that we were still reading together in Jerusalem, "*Du sei wie du, immer*" ["You be like you, always"] is not a simple poem. We spoke a great deal about it, but it was a talk *with* the poem and not *about* the poem.

NM: How important was silence?

IS: Sometimes we found moments of silence, of supreme, genuine silence. Unfortunately, I am mostly rather restless and talkative. In Jerusalem and in Paris we talked like crazy, told story after story. When he became silent, he was mainly ill-tempered, angry. For no reason in particular. It came suddenly, clear out of the blue.

NM: A darkness.

IS: One can call it darkness, but he would suddenly become angry because I'd spoiled something, said something wrong, behaved badly. For example, the first night in Paris. All at once he was enraged, stopped speaking, kept silent a long time. Later on it came to light that I had been distracted by the surroundings and had looked off in another direction while he was talking to me.

NM: You knew him very well, even when he was still very young. Do you believe that he found his subject, his all important subject, suffering, through the Holocaust, with the Holocaust—that he had been waiting for a great, sorrowful subject, and that subject came to him through Fate?

IS: I thought I knew him well. Paul was really quite contemplative from childhood on and always bore a certain sadness within himself. At the same time he was capricious and could quite suddenly become merry and high-spirited. He sensed his great nervous collapse coming on, but he had always had sorrow within himself, before it came to us. From youth onward, for him it was an existential problem. When his parents were deported, he was in despair, had terrible feelings of guilt. It was very difficult for him to speak about it; he felt alone.

NM: Melancholic?

IS: Yes, depressed. He also spoke of suicide.

NM: Already at that time?

IS: Yes, he spoke of suicide. When my sister committed suicide, again and again we spoke about death and the need to say farewell. He said only a little about his parents, nevertheless the burden was always present.

NM: Then I ask myself, whether these themes, such deep and important ones—suffering, death, annihilation—were not already obsessive themes, reiterated and becoming stronger for his soul and mind, at that bleak "right" moment of horror, in the right phase of his writing.

IS: That's difficult to say—it's also a perilous notion. I don't like to hear people say that Celan is "the poet of the Holocaust," because I don't believe it. He is *also* that. The word is there, although he never pronounces it, quite consciously. Because for him there is no word for it. Judaism is there; Jesus is there; Love is there; the Cosmos is there. All and Nothing. He is called the Jew, the Poet, the One Who Got Away [*der Davongekommene*]. But he did not get away. He could not escape. He carried what is historic and what is Judaic within himself, as I said earlier. From youth onward, for him it was both personal and existential experience. His writing was his life—experience and writing were ONE for him.

NM: Do you think if you had succeeded in getting to Paris two or three days before his suicide that it would have been possible to save him?

IS: Perhaps for that moment it would have been possible.

NM: Where did you get that feeling, where does it come from?

IS: It was his last letter. I also spoke with him on the telephone; and then after the final letter I tried to call him again, but there was no answer. When I was about to leave Paris, in a previous visit he wrote down the address of one of his close friends, and he said to me in Yiddish, "*Ojf nischt zu bedarfn* [Even if useless/even if not to be used]. Surely you know how things are with me." While friends were looking for him, his cleaning lady knew that "une Madame d'Israel" would arrive. Thus he knew intuitively that I would come. When I arrived, I met Gisèle [Celan's wife] at his friend's place. Paul's name in Hebrew was "Pessach." It was just on Passover Evening that Paul disappeared. When Paul once told me quite mysteriously that his Jewish name was "Pessach," he added: "Sounds too Jewish, doesn't it!" We laughed.

NM: You said that the relationship—though it was always important and deep—became even more important after his death. For you and for your husband. And that it took on additional significance.

IS: Yes, the relationship expanded, deepened, and new aspects and perspectives came into play. Concerning my husband, he had a great deal of understanding for me and for what happened to me and to us, but in the end he had his limits.

NM: It gets to a point. And then comes the explosion.

IS: The explosion came, and it was difficult. We had a great deal of tolerance for each other, but there was also ambivalence and conflicts that were difficult to endure. We had to spend some time living apart.

NM: A long time?

IS: A few years. For awhile I lived alone with my daughter.

NM: And your daughter, how did she cope with this?

IS: She, too, had a lot of understanding, but which subliminally made things difficult for both of us. Back then—she was between fifteen and seventeen—it was only natural. My daughter and my grandchildren are also tolerant now. For example, I asked them, too, for their opinion about the publication of the correspondence. They told me that my doubts were exaggerated and that publication is important. Of course I should publish the book.

NM: I suspect there is also a great deal of love for her mother.

IS: My daughter? Perhaps, but she loved and admired her father without reservation. With me, she has had many more conversations; we have spent more time together. Nevertheless, we often had mother-daughter conflicts. So, it was not easy, at the time. Michaela did a lot of crazy things back then. She was in Gymnasium and should have taken her graduation exam, but she did not want to learn.

NM: So, was she, too, in a particular period of her life?

IS: Yes, even my daughter and my husband had their difficulties and were rather complicated, quite separately from me. My husband was not easy to comprehend. He appeared to be balanced, dependable, extremely courteous, earnest and successful, and this was not entirely the case. It wasn't really that he pretended, he just made the impression. He had a lot of charm, and everyone liked him, people held him in high esteem. In our circle of friends my relationship with Celan was really taken very badly.

NM: Yes, it was a time of great tension, but what do you think today about the mythology surrounding Celan? A mythology always arises around an artist. A mythology that exaggerates or alters [its subject].

IS: Or places an official stamp on it.

NM: In what way have you felt this?

IS:
Celan basically was and remained a spoiled little mama's boy from Czernowitz—this I believe only a few knew and saw through.

NM: Yes, you said that to me. A typical one?

IS: Typical. After all, one of the many such children. (I am not now alluding, of course, to his also truly unspeakable gifts.) But in Czernowitz, there was something of a cult of genius. Every second or third child was a genius from whom infinitely much was expected. You, yourself, as well as the others, those less gifted, had to suffer this. And what was genius? That was not so precisely defined. A little talent in figure skating or playing the piano, the ability to speak many languages, especially to "parlez français," study abroad. In Jewish families, this was the case most everywhere. But parents in Czernowitz were insatiable. They wanted the best and meant well; yet in many cases nothing good came of it.

NM: I asked you about the mythology, the image that posterity has made of him. I don't much like it when a great production is made of it all, with the mythology of posterity, posterity as theater.

IS: Yes, there is something like the posthumous history of the great minds, of the artists, etc. There's an afterlife, a kind of iconography, which can become part of each one's fictitious biography. For that very reason, in the case of Celan, I long had to contemplate, to read and reread him again and again, to search and try to pare away the rind to get to what seems true.

The many images of Celan: Celan the dark, stooped man of sorrows . . . Celan, poet of the Shoah . . . Celan the deranged man. . . the sick man . . . the mystic . . . the master . . . the womanizer . . . the counterfeiter and plagiarist . . . the poseur . . . the empty man, the silenced man . . . and yet, and yet, and yet . . . Celan, a genuine poet.

NM: But let's return to his sensitivity as a child.

IS: There was much talk of his bad father who lacked understanding— and of his loving, giving, angelic, and admiring mother. Like most children, Paul received thrashings. Other children simply dealt with them as a matter of course. Paul was more hurt, because he was more sensitive. But what exactly was the nature of his sensitivity? Later the problems Celan had with his father were compared to those Kafka had

146

with his—also a myth. Celan's genius, if one may call it that, was a gift of the gods, and thus the heaviest burden. He felt no one understood him. It could be no other way. He did not endure the loneliness that must have arisen out of this. And besides, perhaps his case is similar to that of Kafka and Benjamin—more and more research always being done at universities and more connections being drawn between them.

NM: Step by step it becomes an academic subject.

IS: But it concerns something else. It must, in their case, be something completely different from an academic debate.

NM: That's why I so enjoy your writing, too, because it is authentic. Sometimes it's also sarcastic and ironic, and I like that very much. Even for the mythology of the Holocaust. Because a great, a huge distortion ensues.

IS: These festivals, these fake Holocaust festivals, evading the subject of memory as a career!

NM: It becomes a ritual, and it becomes theater, almost.

IS: Were it a real, an authentic ritual, which had grown out of experience, it could be valuable, but as it has been handled it is something else. It is business, politics as usual, manipulated by vested interests.

NM: There are so many repetitions, so many rehearsals, until finally the performance is completely artificial, the original notion meaningless.

IS: One becomes blunted, indifferent. Whether and how Celan gets falsified is an open question. What is the significance of Jewishness in his poetry? Was it the "*Anders-sein*" ["otherness"]? Was it the quotation from Tsvetaeva, "All poets are Jews"? On the one hand he was occupied with Levinas; on the other hand, the dispute with Heidegger was very important. This is already difficult to accept.

NM: The Heidegger affair?

IS: Yes, another affair, which disturbed him, about which we also spoke often. Celan was under the spell of Heidegger's language —of *Being and Time*, of concepts like *"Geworfen-Sein"* ["being thrown"]. In the end, Celan felt wounded by Heidegger, although the latter took great interest in Celan.

NM: He was a wholly great authority.

IS: I heard a lot of contradictory information about their final meeting in March 1970 in Freiburg—what Celan wrote to me and what Professor Baumann reports about this encounter. Celan wrote to me that Heidegger did not understand him. Baumann says the opposite: Heidegger listened with complete attention and afterward even recited something by heart. Heidegger had seen Celan out as far as the gate, then he returned to his other guests and said, "Celan is very, very sick." According to Baumann.

NM: Yes, this is strange.

IS: Celan's so-called "illness" and his stays in French psychiatric care were very bad. Treatment was conventional—not sophisticated.

NM: And today?

IS: About the present time I do not know. But in his time, when he told me about it, it sounded terrible. Of course there were also very good psychiatrists in Paris, but he did not get to them. Nor did he want to.

NM: I'm convinced he did not want to. Did he have this "inner" need for Jerusalem, the "center" missing from his life, in his life as a poet? As an imagined center for his feeling and thinking, not necessary for living in it? An inner, symbolical location, a poetical, lyrical stimulus? Was he experiencing a spiritual need to return to Jerusalem? You told me that he had the notion that you were the daughter of Zion.

IS: That was a bit of an exaggeration. We also laughed about it!

NM: Exactly, but for him, Jerusalem became, so to speak, a metaphorical necessity—dreamy, a lost and absent destination?

IS: A dream of "Heavenly Jerusalem," but also the opposite. There are, among others, two poems about Jerusalem. In one of them, Jerusalem is in the light, *"Das Leuchten"* [The Shining]—that rides toward us: the radiance that approaches "from temples' depths." Then, in the counter-poem, Jerusalem, *"Tochtergeschwulst einer Blendung im All"* [daughter metastasis of a glare in space], Jerusalem is a cancer. He wrote those two poems on one and the same day, "The Shining" and "Daughter metastasis of a glare in space." Two oppositional imaginings of Jerusalem.

NM: You also mentioned provincialism.

IS: Israel is provincial.

NM: Even if international conferences with many people take place, in the end there is still provincialism; they end with highly provincial rhetoric. And here is the split between us and the others.

IS: There is also the opposite. We have very many talented writers in Israel.

NM: And with a vision that is much broader and, one can say, universal. There is now a generation of artists and authors who are more at home in the world, not only here.

IS: The world can be provincial, too.

NM: The world is becoming a small village.

I read the little book about your family and upbringing. I find it interesting that you were in this affluent environment, and that as a child and even later, you never found it easy to endure. You were and you remained, I am convinced, far more authentic and on the left.

IS: Whatever that means.

NM: What this means today we no longer know. But what it meant at that time, we do know, and I ask myself whether, when the Russians arrived—you suffered through that, did you not?

IS: Principally that affected my parents. In the beginning, I did not sufficiently suffer with them in the same way, as I was a very young girl back then.

NM: Your parents and also you, for there was a connection. One cannot deny this. Did one then suddenly understand, things are not as one dreamed, things are different?

IS: About Stalin one already knew beforehand what the reality looked like. But the whole extent of the danger was not clear to us. With the Germans, it happened in a very similar way. My father, for example, took the German occupation better than the Soviet, even though we were in greater danger. During the time of the Soviet occupation, many Jews denounced one another, slandered one another, wanting to protect themselves at other people's expense. There was little loyalty among Jews. My father suffered greatly because of that.

NM: Was there no loyalty then?

IS: Among us, there is often a poor show of loyalty.

NM: And the Jewish Communists—

IS: —were also in jeopardy. Even more than the non-communists.

NM: Were there many?

IS: Comparatively. There were the young, and a whole crowd of drawing-room Communists. On the other side there were the Zionists, the Yiddishists, the Bundists, and others—businessmen and academics, who considered themselves citizens of the world and wanted to go to the West, to America. Celan, for example, as a fourteen- or fifteen-year-old was very active as a Communist. He, too, contributed writing to their illegal newspaper. But long before the invasion of the Russians, he recognized Stalin and withdrew from active participation in Communism. He stuck by his friends from that time, however, and later, too, he wrote and sent letters on to them in the "East." When the Soviets moved in, I remember meeting him on the street. I asked him, "Now what do you think?"

"Now I'm an Anarchist," he replied.

This was already dangerous. At the university, too, he had represented himself as "anarchistic." He kept to his leftist stance. At the time of the student uprisings in Paris he got up on the barricades. Once, late in the evening, he got hungry. He asked a comrade if he thought he would be able to find an open restaurant. "What are you thinking about? We are in the middle of a revolution! *Et tu ne pense qu'a bouffer!*" Then Paul thought, now it's time for him to make his retreat.

NM: And here in Israel you were more or less on the left, no? Rather suddenly.

IS: Yes, but I was not really active—I never belonged to a party.

NM: No, not actively. But in your thoughts?

IS: In my thoughts . . . for example, I'm thinking of the Eichmann trial and the incomprehension of the majority of Israelis, who thought only in black and white, who could never show any understanding whatsoever for Hannah Arendt's attitude. The petition of Buber, [Samuel Hugo] Bergman, and a few other intellectuals moved me in particular, also of my good friend the painter Yehuda Bacon. Do you know of him?

NM: No.

IS: Today he is an Israeli painter; he comes from Prague. As a child he was in Theresienstadt and Auschwitz and lost his family, survived and came to Israel at roughly eighteen years of age. Buber and Bergmann took care of him; he found a home with Bergman, and he got support for his study of painting at Bezalel. Yehuda was a witness at the Eichmann trial. As a youth, he carried the dead out of the gas chambers, that was his job. He survived Auschwitz, and now along with Buber, Bergman and other intellectuals, he signed the petition against the death sentence that would hang Eichmann.

NM: Ah, I did not know this. Really?

IS: Yes, the government and the media swept it under the rug.

NM: Why was that?

IS: It's clear. I believe that in Bergman's diaries one could find a more precise account.

NM: How did you follow the trial?

IS: I am ashamed to confess that I did not closely follow the trial. For me, I believe it was already, as always, hard to deal with what one calls Shoah among us—yet neither would I know how to deal with it any better.

NM: Yes, I understand this very well. I too.

IS: On the other hand I cannot—and I do not—want to forget, either. But I cannot hate. I cannot hate the Germans. I experience and understand all of what happened, in a broad context, not as the responsibility of *one* person or *one* people. I want to learn to comprehend, if one can actually speak of comprehension. But I have no feelings of hatred. Neither do I feel myself to be a victim, although in a certain sense I was—the yellow star, displaced, disenfranchised, and humiliated. I have the feeling of not having suffered equivalent pain; no hunger, no freezing cold, no torments in a camp. This [sense of] survival at-the-edge is excruciating and persists.

NM: And your relationship to the German language? Surely it is far deeper and more important than the one you have to Hebrew?

IS: It's different. Unfortunately, I never immersed myself in the Hebrew language. When I first came here, the Ulpan did not exist, and I had to study privately. When I was in the seminar on music education and later, in my advanced studies, of course I spoke Hebrew and wrote in Hebrew, but it was rather functional, in connection with my studies. I learned a great deal from my husband, who spoke Hebrew exceptionally well.

NM: How come?

IS: He arrived in the country at the age of thirteen, and he had a gift for learning languages.

NM: From Switzerland?

IS: From Turkey, from Istanbul.

NM: From Istanbul?

IS: He was born in Istanbul and went to a German school. But his parents spoke no German. His father came from Ukraine and his mother's family from Bessarabia. They wanted to emigrate to America. Hermann, my future husband, was the only one in the family who went to the German school and spoke German. He loved both the language and the school very much. He absorbed German from kindergarten on. He told me how he had played his role as a little dwarf in Snow White and the Seven Dwarves. He still knew it by heart. He was a superior student and won prizes—I still own an edition of the Grimms' *Fairy Tales* from that time. He brought his entire German library to Palestine. With his pocket money he bought more antiquarian books in German. He translated Karl May and [Theodor] Storm into Hebrew, for example, "The City on the Sea." For him, Tel Aviv was the city on the sea. So, at thirteen he was already a German romantic.

NM: How was the relationship with the Romanians? Did you have one?

IS: Scarcely at all, on my part. I went to private schools, where there were no Romanian girls. My father had Romanian friends. He also had a Romanian partner in the factory.

NM: No contact whatsoever?

IS: Very little. Except for with the maid.

NM: And how did the Romanians act then?

IS: Then, during the war? I can recall Romanian officers who helped us without asking anything in return. Readiness to help. . . ?

153

NM: This was in '41, right?

IS: From '40-'41 till '44, we knew a Romanian officer, who by chance, when we had to move into the ghetto, would travel to Arad, where one of my mother's aunts lived. My mother had the idea of filling a big wardrobe-trunk with objects she was fond of, giving it to him, and asking him to take it along with him. We could not take things along with us in any case, naturally. She packed up all the following: books and letters and pictures and silver and cutlery and small objects of art. I still have a few things from there with me in my home today. For example, the silver sugar bowl my mother brought as part of her dowry from Vienna. Also this little mosaic frame. These two pictures our architect painted of our factory, the entrance to the factory. They come from the early thirties. I also have letters from my grandmother to my mother, in gothic script, and many extremely old photographs.

NM: And the officer took it along with him?

IS: My mother managed to pack it all into a gigantic wardrobe-trunk, as marvelously as she could. I can still remember that none of the porcelain broke on the long journey. It was sent with good luck, and the Romanian officer delivered it honestly and loyally.

NM: And he demanded nothing at all in return?

IS: Nothing.

NM: That is extraordinary.

IS: Our aunt sent the wardrobe-trunk from Arad to Palestine after the war (circa 1946). It arrived with all its contents.

NM: Is there anything important about Celan, do you think, that has been neglected? For example, arriving in Paris at the right time?

IS: I don't believe it would have changed anything very much had I arrived in Paris at the right time, which of course I hoped to do. No, I don't believe I could have helped him. I believe that his circle, his environment in Paris, was not good for him.

NM: Would it be possible to be together with him for a long while?

IS: No. That was clear to us. We spoke and wrote to each other about that.

NM: This was felt?

IS: He knew, too, that he was "in the long run unbearable," which he also writes. To speak frankly, I am not one of those women who, as the saying goes, can live only for a man. I can be very present, and I can give a lot, too—but I was afraid of not being able to withdraw and simply be there for the other. This pains me greatly concerning Paul; he required it. That I always wanted more—although I assured him of the opposite—more and more letters and attention, this was, I fear, too much of a burden.

NM: Did he take it? This he needed, too?

IS: I know it was childish, that I would have to acquiesce more and not always expect more from him than he could give.

NM: Really?

IS: I needed attention which, at the time, I also received in large part when we were together. He was very attentive, capable of listening and perceiving and understanding in ways one seldom experiences. He really wanted to know, understand, and recognize.

NM: Who is this woman, who is she?

IS: Yes, he wanted really to know and to see. He could also remember everything imaginable from Czernowitz. Once he asked me if my mother was still so childish. He recalled my mother and every possible situation in our house. And it was true, my mother was somewhat childish. A very dear, sweet mother, but also childish and self-centered.

NM: And his relationship to his son? Was there a real connection, or not?

IS: Paul had a mental image of an ideal family. He wanted this in life. It did not work. He asked too much.

NM: Idealistic . . . a sacred image?

IS: A divine image. Later, though, he had real sorrows concerning his son.

NM: The family there was Catholic, but what was he? Jewish?

IS: Eric is neither a Jew nor a Christian. He has no interest in a tradition of any kind. He loves the circus and learned magic and juggling in a circus school.

NM: And how do you remember Gisèle?

IS: When people were searching for Celan in Paris after his suicide, we met at Lutrand's, one of Paul's friends. She did not want to leave me alone in a hotel and invited me to stay with her. We talked the whole night through. It was a good, open conversation, and we drank whisky, which made many things easier. Gisèle was educated in a convent school, but her rebellion against home came principally through her decision to live with Paul. In my opinion, she admired him greatly, but she was also fearful of him. I believe it was difficult for her to accept and to understand his complex personality. She was very magnanimous, very delicate, one could say aristocratic. Paul also accepted this in her. She was prepared to become a Jewess, to go to Israel. She was prepared to do a lot for him, but he did not want this at all. Worlds lay between the two of them.

NM: Everything for him.

IS: But she was a good artist, and Paul enjoyed giving names to her abstract pictures.

NM: How did Gisèle handle his relationships with other women? His affairs?

IS: This question has already been discussed so thoroughly, that I would prefer to refrain from speaking about it. The one thing I have to add is that I did not experience Celan as a typical ladies' man or skirt-chaser. He sought to have genuine relationships and gave a great deal in a relationship.

—Translated from the German by Rika Lesser

Biographical Note

Ilana Shmueli (1924, Czernowitz—2011, Jerusalem)

Ilana Shmueli was born Liane Josephine Schindler in Czernowitz, Romania in 1924. Though the Schindlers survived and remained during WWII, they wore the yellow star and Ilana's sister (known as "Dolly") committed suicide.

Paradoxically, it was in conditions of the most severe repression, under German-Romanian occupation, that Ilana's real education began and flourished. She studied English, French, Latin, Yiddish, and ancient Greek (later in Israel she would also learn Hebrew) along with poetry and the violin. Among a group of keen young people and inspired teachers, she would read Rilke, Trakl, George, and Kraus, and secretly listen to the music of Beethoven. It was during this period that she became close friends with Paul Celan, who read her his early poems on forbidden walks in the park.

In 1944, Ilana and her family emigrated illegally to Palestine. When they arrived in the future state of Israel they were assigned to an internment camp near Haifa, and then settled elsewhere. In 1948, Ilana joined the Israeli army and took part in the war of liberation, working with young immigrants from the DP camps, who were inducted immediately on arrival. Following an early, arranged marriage that resulted in divorce, Ilana married Prof. Dr. Hermann (Herzl) Shmueli in 1953. Their daughter, Michaela, was born in 1956.

In 1965, on a visit to Paris, Ilana looked up Paul Celan. They corresponded, and when Celan made his first and only visit to Israel, in October 1969, they became lovers. An exchange of letters and poems followed (*The Correspondence of Paul Celan & Ilana Shmueli*, The Sheep Meadow Press, 2011). After Celan's suicide in Paris, in April 1970, she began to translate (German-Hebrew and Hebrew-German). Her first translations were of Celan's poems. Some of them appeared, in Hebrew, in Israel in 1999 as part of a slim volume containing her reflections and insights on Celan's work. She also began to write poems of her own in German.

Ilana Shmueli's volumes of prose and poetry:

Denk dir. Paul Celan in Jerusalem (Just Think. Paul Celan in Jerusalem) in *Jüdisches Almanach*, a publication of the Leo Baeck Institute: 1995. An expanded edition, in Hebrew, appeared in 1999 in Israel, with 27 of Celan's poems and excerpts from their correspondence added to the book. The most recent edition, with an afterword by Matthias Fallenstein, was published in 2010 (Aachen: Rimbaud).
Ein Kind aus guter Familie (Child of a Good Family), a memoir (Aachen: Rimbaud, 2006).
Zwischen dem Jetzt und dem Jetzt. Gedichte (Between Now and Now. Poems). (Aachen: Rimbaud, 2007).
Leben im Entwurf. Gedichte (Drafting a Life: Poems). (Aachen: Rimbaud, 2011).

In 2009, Ilana Shmueli was awarded the Theodor Kramer Prize for Writing in Resistance and in Exile.

Just before the outbreak of the Gulf War in 1991, Shmueli decided to bring her correspondence with Paul Celan to safety and gave it, at the request of Celan's widow Gisèle Lestrange, to the German Literary Archive in Marbach. At that time, she published the correspondence which appeared as *Paul Celan/Ilana Shmueli, Briefwechsel* with Suhrkamp Publishers, Frankfurt, in 2004, edited by Ilana Shmueli and Thomas Sparr. An English translation, *The Correspondence of Paul Celan & Ilana Shmueli* (trans. Susan H. Gillespie), appeared in 2011 (The Sheep Meadow Press).

Susan H. Gillespie has translated German philosophy, musicology, memoirs, and poetry. Her translation of *The Correspondence of Paul Celan & Ilana Shmueli* (Sheep Meadow Press, 2011) was a finalist for the National Translation Award. She is the founding director of the Institute for International Liberal Education, Bard College.

Gerald Stern is Gerald Stern.

Norman Manea is Norman Manea. The Sheep Meadow Press has published Norman Manea's conversation with Saul Bellow, *Settling My Accounts Before I Go Away*, and an interview of Norman Manea by Hannes Stein, *Paradise Found*.

Rika Lesser is a poet and translator. Two of her books, *Etruscan Things* and *Questions of Love: New and Selected Poems*, were published by The Sheep Meadow Press.